CULTURAL CRITICISM, LITERARY THEORY, POSTSTRUCTURALISM

CULTURAL CRITICISM, LITERARY THEORY, POSTSTRUCTURALISM

Vincent B. Leitch

Columbia University Press

New York

Columbia University Press
New York   Chichester, West Sussex
Copyright © 1992 Columbia University Press
All rights reserved

Library of Congress CIP Data

Leitch, Vincent B.
    Cultural criticism, literary theory,
  poststructuralism / Vincent B. Leitch.
        p.   cm.
    Includes bibliographical references and index.
    ISBN 0-231-07970-2 (alk. paper)
    ISBN 0-231-07971-0 (pbk.)
    1. Criticism—History—20th century.
  2. Poststructuralism (Literary analysis)
    I. Title.
PN94.L39   1992
801'.95'0904—dc20   92-19447
                                        CIP

Casebound editions of Columbia University Press books
are printed on permanent and durable acid-free paper.

Printed in the United States of America

c   10 9 8 7 6 5 4 3 2 1
p   10 9 8 7 6 5 4 3 2 1

CONTENTS

Contents

PREFACE

One remarkable characteristic of contemporary academic literary studies is the diversity of material considered relevant to the enterprise. In addition to the history of languages and canonical literatures, literary intellectuals commonly study and teach such discourses as women's literature, film, folklore, popular culture, myth, minority literatures, rhetoric, theory of criticism, poetics, theater history, television, and postcolonial literatures. Doubtless, scholarly attention to such texts diminishes the centrality of the literary classics, particularly as it shifts focus from the essentials of literariness to social codes, conventions, and representations. Literary works are increasingly regarded as communal documents or as events with social, historical, and political dimensions rather than as autonomous artifacts within an aesthetic domain. The widespread interest in "discourse" as opposed to belletristic "literature" testifies, no doubt, to the expanding social importance of popular culture and mass media and the decreasing status of canonical literature. Significantly, changes have occurred not only in the objects of study but in the methods of analysis. Literary critics frequently call into service sociological, historical, political, and institutional modes of inquiry—without giving up close reading and explication. The turn toward "discourse" as the object of scrutiny and ideological analysis as a main method of investigation bears witness to a resurgence of cultural criticism. The primary objective of this book is to argue for a cultural criticism broadly informed by poststructuralist thinking.

*　　　*　　　*

From the eighteenth century onward, cultural criticism has been preoccupied with the social roles of the arts and intellectuals, the uses of education and literacy, the effects of economic transformation and massification stemming from industrialism, the workings of institutions, the relative status of popular, mass, and canonical cultures, and the possibilities of change. Given such concerns, it is not surprising that cultural critics share interests and methods not only with anthropologists, historians, media specialists, and sociologists but with a wide array of Marxists, semioticians, hermeneuticists, mythographers, feminists, ethnic theorists, and poststructuralists.

One of the preoccupations of cultural critics is the definition of "culture." In current usage the word displays a broad range of designations: it names intellectual and artistic practices, especially literature, music, painting, sculpture, theater, philosophy, and criticism; it describes processes of intellectual, spiritual, aesthetic, and ethical development; it indicates the distinctive way of life of a people or period or humanity as a whole; it signals refinement of taste, judgment, and intellect; and it includes manners, conventions, customs, myths, institutions, and patterns of thought. The polysemy of the word and the perennial contention surrounding the idea reveal less a failure to isolate a discrete object of inquiry than a recurring magnetic pull characteristic of both the concept and the project of studying culture.

The emergence of "cultural studies" in the closing third of the twentieth century signals the advent of a new academic discipline analogous to women's studies and ethnic studies. One distinctive feature of academic cultural studies is a political orientation rooted variously in Marxist, non-Marxist, and post-Marxist leftist intellectual traditions, all critical of the aestheticism, formalism, antihistoricism, and apoliticism common among the dominant methods of literary analysis during the middle third of the century. Advocates of cultural studies are predisposed to intervene actively in issues of social struggle. In their analyses of such contemporary items as fashions, films, magazines, photographs, romances, and subcultural groups, scholars of cultural studies attend to phases of consumption and distribution as well as production, isolating forces of commodification and resistance, hegemony and subversion. Within the long tradition of cultural criticism, the relatively recent formation of cultural studies, especially in Britain during the 1970s, constitutes a significant moment of flowering and institutionalization, but one not without problems, as chapter 8 illustrates.

*   *   *

Several noteworthy shifts regarding cultural criticism occurred within academic literary circles between the 1930s and 1960s. A taboo against engaging in cultural criticism was encouraged and enforced by formalists, particularly in the immediate postwar period. This taboo was undermined during the 1960s, first by myth critics, ethnic intellectuals, New Leftists, and feminists, and then by numerous others, including mainstream liberals. During the time of the second transition the practice of cultural critique increasingly challenged the taboo on cultural inquiry, revealing a shift in interest to ethics, politics, and social activism.

I want to recall briefly some formulations of the taboo in order to retrieve key conditions of possibility for contemporary cultural criticism. In his celebrated article "A Critic's Job of Work," Blackmur excoriated various heretical approaches to criticism, namely so-called moralism, sociologism, and psychologism. Blackmur championed "unindoctrinated thinking" and the "absence of positive doctrine," recommending as essential to criticism "imaginative skepticism and dramatic irony" (375–76). With Blackmur, as with other formalist theorists, "criticism must be concerned, first and last—whatever comes between—with the poem as it is read and as what it represents is felt" (390).

A parallel denigration of so-called extrinsic critical approaches was also promoted during the mid-thirties by Crane, leader of the Chicago school:

> The essential thing about the understanding to which the literary critic aspires is that it is understanding of literary works in their character as works of art. It is not criticism but psychology when we treat poems or novels as case books and attempt to discover in them not the art but the personality of their authors. It is not criticism but history or sociology when we read imaginative writings for what they may tell us about the manner or thought or "spirit" of the age which produced them. It is not criticism but ethical culture

when we use them primarily as a means of enlarging and enriching
our experience of life or of inculcating moral ideas. . . . Criticism
. . . is simply the disciplined consideration, at once analytical and
evaluative, of literary works as works of art. (12)

Like other formalist theorists, Crane advocated aesthetic criticism—
criticism of works of art as crafted works of art. The centripetal or
tautological thrust of such an endeavor manifested itself in a sometimes puritanical purge of so-called nonaesthetic modes, particularly
of psychological, sociological, and moral criticism, all of which appeared heretical activities for leading Chicago critics and New Critics
alike.

As crystalized in Wellek and Warren's influential *Theory of Literature,* the formalist stance in literary criticism required the unequivocal
centrality of immanent aesthetic analysis: "The study of literature
should, first and foremost, concentrate on the actual works of art
themselves" (139). Such positive concentration ruled out certain dangerous tendencies. "What literature is, by modern definition, 'pure
of' is practical intent (propaganda, incitation to direct, immediate action) and scientific intent (provision of information, facts, 'additions
to knowledge')" (239). In essence, the formalist project of purifying
literature set politics and ethics as well as science and philosophy outside the bounds of proper critical concern. This narrowing of literary
criticism and theory became a privileged strategy characteristic of
an era.

It would be easy enough to multiply the examples of the extremist
"purge mentality" of certain major formalist critics. It would also be
possible to demonstrate that some leading erstwhile formalists de-
parted from the puritanical program. Even in the heyday of the thirties and forties, critics like Burke, Eliot, Empson, and Winters "in-
dulged" in social, historical, political, and ethical criticism. Despite
various exceptions, however, a taboo on cultural criticism long ex-
isted in academic literary circles and in diminished scope persists today.

Like all taboos, such an injunction replicates the formula "thou shalt not ————————————," thereby reproducing the most basic of ethicopolitical acts. Accordingly, the more formalistic a critical project would be, the more rigorously it would adhere to a particular party line, operating in the wake of an obsessive value. If there ever was an example of unskeptically flying under a banner or of serving a doctrine, this is it. Amplifying and reversing Crane, I would argue that it is not criticism but self-deluding aesthetic dogmatism when literary theorists restrict criticism to studying literature for literature's sake. Although indistinctly, this dogmatism embodies an ethics of disinterest and disengagement contemptuous of worldly matters while committed to the secular spiritualizing of art.

*   *   *

However multifaceted and heterogeneous it is, poststructuralism in most of its guises exhibits certain distinctive traits, including rejection of reason as universal or foundational; problematization of linguistic reference and textual interpretation; decentering of the subject; suspicion of totalizing narratives; affirmation of the nexus of knowledge/interest/power; criticism of modernity and the legacy of the Enlightenment; stress on history and culture as discursive constructions and sites of struggle; interrogation of established disciplinary and intellectual boundaries; and sensitivity to differences, exclusions, anomalies, and margins.

Unlike formalism, which characteristically succumbs to the temptation to purify, poststructuralism tends to construe entities as entangled in complicated networks. This explains in part why the catalog is a recurring stylistic feature of this book. Incomplete and disjunctive, catalogs stand in for unified totalities. For poststructuralists texts are always already multitrack intertexts. In the beginning was the polylogue, socially situated and heteroglot.

Poststructuralism, like neopragmatism, collapses the traditional theory/practice distinction, framing "theory" as one mode of practice, neither transcendental nor privileged. Theory is not superior or prior to practice. None of this, however, spells the end of theorizing; it revalues and resituates theory. Among literary scholars and critics there are numerous practices, and literary theory represents only a small segment of a complex field. At certain historical times and places close reading (so-called practical criticism) has held sway, giving rise to an antitheoretical ethos. At other moments and sites "theory" has held pride of place over practice. In both cases, it is not a matter of epistemology, but of the history and sociology of knowledge. This book scrutinizes theories, develops practices, and propounds countertheoretical practices. Instead of examining films, novels, plays, or poems, it analyzes and assesses critical, speculative, and practical essays, tracts, and disquisitions, attending to the intellectual "foundations" of contemporary criticism; to the linkages, circulations, and functions of certain key concepts; and to the ethicopolitical ramifications of institutionalized practices, theories, and organizations of knowledge. Such "theorizing" of criticism involves practicing cultural criticism.

While literary critics have long engaged in cultural theory and criticism, not all cultural critics have dwelt on literary matters. Literary and cultural criticism are not identical; they share areas of overlap. It is possible for literary intellectuals to undertake cultural criticism without giving up literary interests. All this would not need saying except that some contemporary advocates of cultural studies, located mainly in literature departments but alienated from literary studies, insist that cultural criticism focus on mass and popular culture and renounce literary discourse and literary theory as narrow and privileged. For cultural critics with literary orientations a certain strategic choice here emerges between transforming literary studies or switching allegiance to cultural studies (conceived by its advocates as a separate and better discipline). I do not think that cultural studies supersedes literary studies, but there are those who strongly disagree, especially among some followers of the Birmingham school. The central role of literary studies in the life of Western societies cannot so easily be dismissed. Although it is an undertaking marked by telling tensions and certain contradictions, the transformation of literary studies strikes me as a worthwhile endeavor. It is a project well under way and poststructuralism has a crucial role to play, as this book demonstrates. The choice between literary and cultural studies is best conceived as both/and, not either/or.

*   *   *

In an earlier book, *American Literary Criticism from the Thirties to the Eighties,* I offered historical narratives of various critical movements and schools that have led to recent developments in cultural criticism. I do not propose to repeat such material in this work. I wish instead to advance the enterprise of poststructuralist cultural criticism. The purpose of this text is to provide not comprehensive historical scholarship but theoretically oriented argumentation, promoting its project mainly by arguing against current influential contending accounts of important issues and problems. Over the course of eight chapters, I develop positions on certain key topics: social formation and cultural critique, authorship and intention, "poetic" discourse and the social text, literary genre and cultural convention, minority literatures and "general poetics," textual interpretation and assessment, institutional theory and analysis, and Birmingham cultural studies and poststructuralism. In constructing my positions, I draw on the work of roughly a dozen poststructuralists, whom I also do not hesitate to criticize. As I made clear in a previous book, *Deconstructive Criticism,* which is an intellectual history of first-generation poststructuralists, the poststructuralist movement has diverse factions and subgroups that in recent years have continued to proliferate. The present work enacts a pragmatic blend of various poststructuralisms, creating a hybrid.

Despite some continuities of subject matter and theme, I hesitate to cast this text as the third work of a trilogy on contemporary critical theory. The earlier historical and comparativist works attempted to be comprehensive and to avoid explicit position taking. While the current book extends the knowledge built up in the former ones, it is polemical in nature, progressing through refutations of selected influential figures. As a manifesto writer, I rely on incisively etched cameos and silhouettes to portray opposing positions. This tactic produces an authoritative tone, but the text is not meant as an authoritarian overview: it is instead an interested intervention in a dense field of argumentation. I concentrate largely on leading theorists because on key issues they have set the terms of debate—for good or ill. With regard to my occasional attacks on New Criticism, I do not conceive such efforts as "whipping a dead horse." On the contrary, since New Criticism's passing in the sixties, it has become immortalized in many places unconsciously as "normal criticism," meriting continued scrutiny and critique. The past vexes and contours our future.

ACKNOWLEDGMENTS

A few bits and pieces of this book appeared in earlier versions in *Deconstructive Criticism* (New York: Columbia University Press, 1983), *American Literary Criticism from the Thirties to the Eighties* (New York: Columbia University Press, 1988), *Critical Texts* 2 (July 1984), and *Association of Departments of English Bulletin* 90 (Fall 1988). Chapter 4 was previously published in *Genre* 24 (Spring 1991) and chapter 8 in *Journal of the Midwest Modern Language Association* 24 (Spring 1991). I thank the editors and publishers for permission to reprint.

Some of my ideas were initially presented in formal lectures at various places, including the Midwest summer session of the Association of Departments of English in 1987, the Center for Twentieth-Century Studies in Milwaukee in 1988, the Department of Comparative Literature of Indiana University in 1988, the annual convention of the South Atlantic Modern Language Association in 1988, the Department of English at Valdosta State College in 1990, Purdue University's Seminar in Rhetoric in 1990, and Memphis State University where I held the Moss Chair in 1991. I appreciate a grant for writing in 1989 provided by Purdue's Center for Humanistic Studies.

1

Analyzing Regimes

It is a well-attested cliché that the functioning of social groups is invariably shaped by "values," which means that certain operative and guiding needs, beliefs, interests, and practices more or less permeate and propel social activities, choices, plans, ideas, customs, and institutions. Taken together, the values within societies constitute material concatenations variously inscribed in law, politics, philosophy, history, ethics, religion, science, education, economics, entertainment, family structures, and aesthetics. As I see it, the conscious and unconscious oppositional and ruling values within social formations, however contradictorily compacted, comprise "regimes of 'reason'" or of "unreason," as the case may be. Aesthetic productions, not surprisingly, partake in such regimes. For good or ill, literary criticism and literature are *cultural* in the sense that they share in regimes of reason operative in societies.

It is worth recalling that contemporary feminist and black literary critics have spent decades opposing sexism and racism, not simply on aesthetic grounds but on moral, political, and economic grounds as well. The obvious point is that "values" operate within and across a complex and dense network of accepted and contested notions, categories, beliefs, conventions, images, and codes. It is no surprise that sexism and racism show up in the court, school, worksite, military, athletic field, prison, press, church/temple/mosque, family, and the arts. Thus, when the New Critics earlier declared the autonomy of poetry and promoted its severance specifically from ethics and politics, they voiced a potent wish, a desperate and alluring desire to enact the "end of ideology," which was a widespread phenomenon in American society that culminated during the immediate postwar years. But despite such fantasies, criticism, like literature, remains tied to regimes of reason; it is regimented and regimenting at the same time.

All this is prologue to my effort as a literary theorist to advocate a project of academic cultural criticism broadly informed by poststructuralist thinking. At the outset of this three-part chapter, I develop further the notion of regimes of reason as an initial substitute for concepts of ideology and social formation. Here I explore the paradoxical connections between analytical totalizing and analytical atomizing, both of which are essential to the enterprise of poststructuralist cultural criticism. Next I sketch what is entailed in the work of poststructuralist cultural critique and how it differs from the main endeavors of formalist literary criticism. Lastly, I initiate critiques of three influential contemporary versions of ethical criticism, including two poststructuralist ones, as a way to conceptualize graphically the entanglements of literary criticism and theory with regimes of reason.

Regimes of Reason

Several characteristics most clearly differentiate the project of cultural criticism from the enterprise of conventional literary analysis. First, cultural criticism attends not simply to canonical literature, but to a whole spectrum of so-called noncanonical and "nonaesthetic" artifacts, phenomena, and discourses. Second, it regularly uses cultural critique and institutional analysis as well as conventional critical methods like textual exegesis and historical background study. And third, what most readily distinguishes poststructuralist cultural criticism from other contending modes is its basic employments of textual and discursive models and procedures derived from researchers such as Barthes, Derrida, and Foucault. For example, Derrida's observation, articulated in *Of Grammatology,* that *"there is nothing outside of the text"* (158) provides a useful protocol for poststructuralist cultural criticism, as do key deconstructive operations of Barthes and certain genealogical conceptualizations of Foucault, as will be evident momentarily and throughout this book.

Here I substitute for the linked concepts of "ideology" and of "social formation" the notion of "regimes of 'reason'" inspired by Foucault's earlier more limited idea, briefly sketched in "Truth and Power," of "regimes of truth." Primarily, I am interested in opening up some useful possibilities to be gained for poststructuralist cultural criticism in its essential work of totalizing and atomizing regimes of reason. If only because the word and concept *ideology* have come in recent times to possess contradictory significations connected with contending political allegiances, I prefer to use regime of reason/unreason to do some of the work of ideology. More important, the notion of regime of reason does not entail commitments to certain problematical Marxian ideas: to the questionable base/superstructure model of social and cultural formation; to the belief that resistance and revolution are uncoded activities; to the vexing view that most socially sanctioned thinking is false consciousness; and to the millenarian certainty about the ultimate direction and victor of history.

To say that cultural criticism engages in cultural critique is to indicate that it regularly scrutinizes and assesses—in its examinations of objects, events, and practices—the often unacknowledged or unnoticed values compacted in regimes of reason, attending to linguistic, ethical, economic, political, historical, philosophical, legal, educational, familial, religious, and aesthetic beliefs, categories, and representations operating in cultural works and activities. While it is possible to engage in such an analytics tied to regimes of reason by using conventional textual exegesis and traditional contextualist history, I advocate poststructuralist methods that treat phenomena as texts linked with other surrounding intertexts and cultural archives. Using the model of the text, one is enabled to conceptualize politics, economics, ethics, and the arts, for instance, as social discourses encoded in archival regimes of reason and open to functionalist analysis and critique.

Significantly, the specificity and density accorded each domain or each discourse forestalls its dissolution back into an all-encompassing, transcendent, encyclopedic REGIME. The intertextual connection of any one specimen text or region of discourse with any other or with many others is not a given, but an arbitrary, though interested, procedure. In the actual processes of investigation, therefore, regimes of reason/unreason appear as coherent, complex, fragmented, or contradictory as an analyst allows. The discourse analysis promoted by cultural criticism aspires to study as many revealing dimensions and facets of regimes of reason as possible—which seemingly commits this project to totalizing modes of inquiry. However, the fundamental poststructuralist principle of infinite intertextuality—not to mention at this point other principles of poststructuralism—undercuts such an aspiration: every analytical rendering is, by definition, partial; a total account could never be made. Since a regime of reason is, in any case, always undergoing processes of formation, having numerous shifting and emergent recesses and margins, it approximates less a monolith than a honeycombed cultural unconscious. At each given moment, contradictions, revisions, and other distortions characterize a regime of reason/unreason, rendering it anything but a massive, centralized, panoptical databank, control center, or *Geist*.

Here an important issue appears, which is crucial to the struggle between poststructuralism and traditional humanism. A brief detour through poststructuralism is helpful in order to extrapolate positive possibilities for cultural criticism. To dramatize the matter, I want to fabricate a simple binary conflict as a way into some complicated issues. In a certain sense the debate between poststructuralism and humanism centers on the liabilities and promises of totalizing versus atomizing modes of understanding and scholarship. Let me cite some examples. Derrida criticizes logocentrism and champions différance, that is, he finds fault with a massive consensus characteristic of Western philosophical culture and opposes to it at numerous turns the disruptive differences flattened out by the reductive installation of logocentrism. A less grandiose version of this conflict occurs in Barthes's study in *S/Z* of Balzac's novella, which in his analysis is segmented into 561 packets of connotation (so-called lexias), all of which are ordered by him arbitrarily into five master codes. Here again an atomizing versus a totalizing operation and, once again, the totalizing activity is explicitly construed as both arbitrary and reductive. In Barthes's words, "If the text is subject to some form, this form is not unitary, architectonic, finite: it is the fragment, the shards, the broken or obliterated network" (20). The strong commitment to critical fragmentation and particularity over against integration and unification is made more explicit when Barthes declares that "the work of the commentary, once it is separated from any ideology of totality, consists precisely in *manhandling* the text, *interrupting* it" (15). Perhaps the height of poststructuralist atomism is reached by de Man in a corrosive aphoristic statement made in "Shelley Disfigured" concerning monumentalizing biographical criticism and cultural history: de Man "warns us that nothing, whether deed, word, thought or text, ever happens in relation, positive or negative, to anything that precedes, follows or exists elsewhere, but only as a random event" (69). This is différance with a vengeance, set in this instance against the factitious unities and connections fostered by acts of writing criticism and history. What I wish to emphasize in all these examples is, first, an obvious tension between atomism and totalization; second, a clear preference among poststructuralists for atomistic fragmentation and decentering; and third, the paradoxical necessity and usefulness among poststructuralists of such totalized entities as logocentrism and history and such totalizing operations as critical writing and codification.

If I were to distill the basic motivating principle of humanism's universalist totalizing mission, it would be "everything is or can be classified." The most extreme impulse of poststructuralist atomism would be "each thing is different," and through cultural practices "relations determine things." Let me briefly catalog some wide-ranging implications of these exaggerated premises. Methodological procedures that serve the unifying goals of humanism include categorizing, thematizing, regularizing, normalizing, synthesizing, integrating, allegorizing, representing, and centralizing. When it is not directly opposed to these operations, poststructuralism is suspicious of such procedures. It prefers fragmenting, differentiating, separating, specifying, randomizing, particularizing, and deconstituting. In this context it is no surprise that the traditional "leading intellectual" is countered by the poststructuralist "specific intellectual"; it could be no other way, as Bové has argued following Foucault. The logical politics of poststructuralism would likely be libertarian communitarianism or anarchism as opposed explicitly to statism or totalitarianism (see Corlett). More forcefully than the community, the state—particularly the modern bureaucratic state—enacts processes of centralization, routinization, and normalization, all of which are anathema to poststructuralism. It is no wonder that what is eccentric, marginal, excluded, "abnormal," or resistant receives sympathetic attention from poststructuralists. It is also not surprising that poststructuralists disavow Marxisms still given to totalizing modes of analysis and organization. Nomadic forms of being and rhizomatous types of affiliation appeal most to poststructuralists. The fragmentations of misreading suit poststructuralism more than fictitious coherencies of "reading." The Foucauldian image of the expanding centralized and omniscient panopticon embodies the worst nightmare of the poststructuralist, as does the more modest image from the Enlightenment of the definitive encyclopedia of knowledge. The various poststructuralist theories of discourse as heteroglossia and polylogue are used directly to counter the concepts of language as univocal, purified, official, Standard. It should be clear why poststructuralism opposes the technologization of psychology and psychoanalysis in such clinical forms as those given to normalizing people and to mechanizing subliminal advertising. Finally, the sociological concept of "ideology," in poststructuralist thinking, is a totalizing encyclopedic idea, associated with various modes of thought in need of rigorous atomistic critique. This explains my advocacy of the atomized/totalized regime of reason—whose underlying methodological premise is "each thing is different but relatable to other things."

The breathtaking scope of much memorable poststructuralist scholarship depends paradoxically on its scrupulous, though highly skeptical, (re)constructions of molar formations like logocentrism, the panopticon, the fashion system, the Scene of Poetic Instruction, and other large-scale structures and cultural discourses characterizing Western societies. For poststructuralist cultural criticism, absorbent "regimes of reason" can serve functions analogous to those above-named systems. Let me concoct a quick hypothetical example. The analysis of a text—say, any one of numerous popular spy novels—might proceed to locate that particular work in the tradition of literary genres, to connect the text with the general purposes of such spy organizations as the CIA and M.I.6, to analyze the roles of advanced technological devices in such books, to assess the goals of master spies and of states supporting them, and to inquire into the representations, where possible, of the family, the school, the court, the church, and the press. One could also, for instance, examine in such novels the revealing minority roles of women, children, Third World people of color, and the elderly. One could compare and contrast television spy shows and novels, attending to what is glorified, what demoted, what dismissed, as well as to what soundtracks, clothing fashions, and interior designs predominate. Let me generalize and restate my main point, a key task of cultural criticism is to link objects of study with regimes of (un)reason. In the hypothetical case at hand, a spy novel is connected to literary history, to military and intelligence establishments, to advanced technology, to the government, to the systems of fashion, interior design, and popular music, and, if practicable, to such institutions as the family, the school, the court, the church, and the media. Characteristically, the specimen text is part of a larger social text, partaking of numerous different discourses, having ties in this case to science and technology, politics and aesthetics, manners and morals, the military and the law—not to mention such institutional representatives as booksellers, publishers, editors, literary agents, television producers, and advertising agents. Entangled in regimes of reason, imbricated in the images and institutions of the culture, embodied in the languages of the "nation," the specimen text is regimented in two senses: first, it is embedded in regimes and, second, it is so embedded, methodologically speaking, through a process of calculated analytical accretions.

Any text may be more or less resistant to cultural hegemony. A whole text or parts of it may contradict, subvert, or refract the reigning culture, just as it or they may confirm, reflect, or support the status quo in the process of helping constitute and circulate it. The specimen work illustrates that for cultural criticism texts are situated within regimes of reason, totalized intertextual molar constructions built up step by step. What the specimen also suggests is how texts can be disconnected and fragmented piece by piece with different segments being scattered hither and yon in atomistic molecular decompositions. One thinks of Barthes's *S/Z*. For poststructuralism every text is a heteroglot hodgepodge compounded of innumerable sources, vocabularies, scripts, traditions, and values—with incompatibilities and discontinuities abounding. This is the burden of readings offered by Derrida, de Man, and Barthes, among others. However paradoxical it seems, the processes of totalizing/atomizing regimes of reason are fundamental to the project of poststructuralist cultural analysis and critique. Without the totalizing operations, regimes of reason do not come into view. Without the atomizing procedures, forces of construction, resistance, transformation, contradiction, subversion, oppression, and change remain obscured.

Poststructuralist Cultural Critique

Whereas a major goal of New Criticism and much other modern formalistic criticism is aesthetic evaluation of freestanding texts, a primary objective of cultural criticism is cultural critique, which entails investigation and assessment of ruling and oppositional beliefs, categories, practices, and representations, inquiring into the causes, constitutions, and consequences as well as the modes of circulation and consumption of linguistic, social, economic, political, historical, ethical, religious, legal, scientific, philosophical, educational, familial, and aesthetic discourses and institutions. In rendering a judgment on an aesthetic artifact, a New Critic privileges such key things as textual coherence and unity, intricacy and complexity, ambiguity and irony, tension and balance, economy and autonomy, literariness and spatial form. In mounting a critique of a cultural "text," an advocate of poststructuralist cultural criticism evaluates such things as degrees of exclusion and inclusion, of complicity and resistance, of domination and letting-be, of abstraction and situatedness, of violence and tolerance, of monologue and polylogue, of quietism and activism, of sameness and otherness, of oppression and emancipation, of centralization and decentralization. Just as the aforementioned system of evaluative criteria underlies the exegetical and judgmental labor of New Criticism, so too does the above named set of commitments undergird the work of poststructuralist cultural critique.

Given its commitments, poststructuralist cultural criticism is, as I have suggested, suspicious of literary formalism. Specifically, the trouble with New Criticism is its inclination to advocate a combination of quietism and asceticism, connoisseurship and exclusiveness, aestheticism and apoliticism. The conservative cultural politics of most New Criticism and its tendency to become reactionary are for obvious reasons anathema to adherents of poststructuralist cultural criticism. Even the evident molecular textual explication and the apparent autonomist poetics promoted by New Critics are of limited use to poststructuralist cultural criticism in its work of atomizing discourse because both are formalist instruments in the service of demonstrating totalized aesthetic coherence and unity. The monotonous practical effect of New Critical reading is to illustrate the subservience of each textual element to a higher, overarching, economical poetic structure without remainders. What should be evident here is that the project of poststructuralist cultural criticism possesses a set of commitments and criteria that enable it to engage in the enterprise of cultural critique. It should also be evident that the cultural ethicopolitics of this enterprise is best characterized, using current terminology, as "liberal" or "leftist," meaning congruent with certain socialist, anarchist, and libertarian ideals, none of which, incidentally, are necessarily Marxian. Such congruence, derived from extrapolating a generalized stance for poststructuralism, constitutes neither a party platform nor an observable course of practical action; avowed tendencies often account for little in the unfolding of practical engagements.

Obviously, my project for contemporary cultural criticism has been influenced and inspired by the work of feminist and ethnic critics, as becomes clearer in succeeding chapters. The powerful specter of sexism and racism as well as opposition to them operating across numerous domains and dimensions of regimes of (un)reason has shown that the work of cultural critique must ultimately be extendable to all facets of cultural discourse. The proclivity of some poststructuralists to remain content with atomizing operations receives a potent corrective in the face of such systematic exclusion and oppression. But the temptation of a poststructuralist analytics to become, therefore, totalizing receives yet another corrective in the face of feminist and ethnic essentialism and separatism: if nothing else, the liberationist celebrations of *écriture féminine* and of negritude, to name just two well-publicized contemporary phenomena, insist on the inescapability and the importance of difference, of otherness, of resistance, of self-determination, and of self-representation. As is well known, the preferred vantage point of poststructuralists is the margin, the place where difference and domination alike characteristically emerge in stark forms. A main job of poststructuralist cultural criticism involves scrutinizing with critical vigilance the concatenations of the multiple margins that constitute regimes of reason.

Ethicopolitical Parameters

The enterprise of cultural criticism entails ethical inquiry. In this domain three of the most influential contemporary attempts at analyzing ethical grounds for academic literary criticism appear in Booth's *Critical Understanding*, Scholes's *Textual Power*, and Miller's *The Ethics of Reading*, all of which are useful though limited.

About his broad project of "critical pluralism" Booth unequivocally asserts that it depends on three binding fundamental values—*understanding*, *justice*, and *vitality*. According to Booth, *understanding* happens when a critic can reconstruct the text of another so that the other can recognize the reconstruction. This activity requires self-surrender. *Justice* occurs when each citizen-critic in the republic of letters is given her or his due according to some specified communal or uniform standard or law. *Vitality* designates enhanced well-being that comes about in the community of critics through the work of criticism. Booth is quite willing to condemn any criticism that sacrifices understanding, justice, or vitality in whatever name. Significantly, he affirms that "texts offered by many authors will enslave us if we succumb to their wishes" (272). Thus, he recommends the crucial practice of "overstanding," that is, the self-assertive act of repudiation, attack, correction, or condemnation. This is critique. The one precondition of Booth's overstanding is that it be preceded by understanding. Ultimately, Booth's project aims to reduce the amounts of willfulness, self-assertion, violence, and misunderstanding that occur within the community of literary critics. "Wherever understanding is maimed, our life is threatened; wherever it is achieved, our life is enhanced" (349).

Among the problems with Booth's enterprise is, to begin with, his lack of interest in "overstanding" the canon whose racism, sexism, and class bias do not comport with the values of social justice, vitality, and understanding. Second, he argues for understanding as a "universal norm," which does not square with the heterogeneous activities of contending interpretive communities. Third, he pegs his concept of understanding to the availability of textual intention: this attempt to delimit the play of meaning rigs the hermeneutic game with the result that certain enigmas of understanding are mitigated at the outset. Fourth, he sets up his ethics of criticism, oddly believing that "it is important for this inquiry to derive our values from within the enterprise of criticism, so that we need not finally appeal to any moral standard other than those that follow from our shared desire for good criticism" (228*n*). This roomy version of "intrinsic" criticism reveals the deductive, wishful nature of Booth's effort. In fact, he does not consider the institutional matrices and values of literary criticism. This skirting of inductive method results because, ironically, he judges the existing site of academic criticism to be a horrid battlefield best avoided. As far as he is concerned, social values should not infiltrate critical values.

A poststructuralist attempt at formulating an explicit ethical project for criticism appears in Scholes's *Textual Power,* a book that gained awards from the MLA and the NCTE and a considerable number of admirers among academic literary intellectuals. Scholes defines three related skills that together constitute critical competence—*reading, interpretation, criticism. Reading* entails discovery of meaning based on familiarity with generic codes and literary-historical contexts. *Interpretation* occurs when reading fails—for example, when an image or passage is opaque or, in another common example, when a partially concealed aspect or level of meaning begins to emerge. Typically, interpretation comes about on account of some excess in a text or some lack in a reader. Whereas reading happens in the realm of the said, interpretation occurs in the domain of the implied, the unsaid, or the repressed. While *criticism* conventionally designates the judicious assessment of a text's fulfilling generic expectations or cultural standards, for Scholes it involves specifically a critique of codes or literary themes, as, for instance, when a feminist uncovers a recurring misogynistic image in a text or in a tradition. Fundamental to criticism are the existence and the exertion of collective and/or class interests and values against the interests and values of a text. As Scholes observes, "Criticism is always made on behalf of a group" (24). Like Booth's overstanding, Scholes's criticism ultimately brings into play a life-enhancing ethicopolitical activity through explicit nay-saying. This is critique. Straightforwardly, Scholes calls for an end to the formalist tradition of "disinterested," "unindoctrinated," "amoral" criticism. "The whole point of my argument is that we must open the way between the literary and verbal text and the social text in which we live. It is only by breaking the hermetic seal around the literary text—which is the heritage of modernism and New Critical exegesis—that we can find our proper function as teachers once again" (24).

Significantly, Scholes develops a fundamental principle of poststructuralist cultural criticism, namely, text is social text. The linguistic, social, and literary codes and conventions embodied in or constitutive of a language give form and shape to texts. Texts come in the wake of communal languages and traditions. The aesthetics of formalist ideology hides such root systems, dehistoricizing and desocializing literature. It is precisely this narrowing of literature and privatizing of criticism that Scholes self-consciously works against with his presentation of criticism as class or collectivist critique. Just as text is linked indissolubly with social body, so criticism is rooted in community. Aesthetics is not severed from ethics or politics. Thus, the task of literary study is not simply aesthetic scrutiny in the pursuit of appreciation and refinement but cultural analysis in the interest of social understanding and human emancipation.

Among the weaknesses of Scholes's project is the seriously misleading implication that reading, interpretation, and criticism occur in three different zones and involve three distinct operations. Scholes evidently knows better but is led to this misapprehension since the overarching context of pedagogy seems to require it. At the point at which Scholes's strong desire for systematic and workable pedagogy distorts matters, it is imprudent for him to let pedagogy rule uncontested. The possibility that the "pedagogization" of criticism and theory may limit or weaken cultural study should not be dismissed, as it largely is by Scholes in *Textual Power*. My argument is that ethics and politics do not simply come in during the closing seconds of the labor of criticism. At the moment discourse is encountered, the values and interests of readers, of texts, and of communities are engaged and operating. It is perfectly possible that I or you might commence a critique, however inchoately, after reading only the first paragraph of a long novel. As readers, we do not progress from linguistic to aesthetic to ethical to political activity in a serial and ascending fashion. From the outset ethicopolitics is part of the critical transaction, despite what both Scholes and Booth suggest.

The logical other side of the poststructuralist idea "text is social text" must be something like "criticism is ethical criticism," which is a proposition explored by Miller in *The Ethics of Reading*. Put briefly, Miller's poststructuralist premise is that language is the inescapable

ground of existence and, therefore, that *reading* constitutes a fundamental human activity. Such reading, however, is "genuine" or
"good" only when it accepts both the necessity and the (paradoxical)
impossibility of moving from textual to "extratextual" realms. Only
through the relay of "difference" (or "différance") are language and
reading linked to an outside reality. Just as the relation between language and reality entails unavoidable detour or deferral, so the connection between reading and text requires inescapable deviation. This
is what Miller calls "the law of the ethics of reading," a fundamental
linguistic rather than an ontological, epistemological, transcendental, or moral necessity.

> It is impossible to get outside the limits of language by means of
> language. Everything we reach that seems outside language, for ex-
> ample sensation and perception, turns out to be more language. To
> live is to read, or rather to commit again and again the failure to
> read which is the human lot. We are hard at work trying to fulfill
> the impossible task of reading from the moment we are born until
> the moment we die. . . . Each reading is, strictly speaking, ethi-
> cal, in the sense that it *has* to take place, by an implacable necessity,
> as the response to a categorical demand, and in the sense that the
> reader must take responsibility for it and for its consequences in the
> personal, social, and political worlds. (59)

What renders *reading* ethical for Miller is a double determination:
first, language requires that we attempt to interpret it; second, ven-
tured interpretations, though inherently deviant, have consequences
for which we readers are responsible. By definition, therefore, criticism is ethical activity. Readers are responsible agents at the mercy of
linguistic necessity.

Although Miller affirms criticism as a cultural activity, there are
serious problems with his endeavor. On the opening page of his first
chapter, he argues that "there is a necessary ethical moment in that act
of reading as such, a moment neither cognitive, nor political, nor social, nor interpersonal, but properly and independently ethical" (1).
This moment of pure or proper "ethicity," uncontaminated by self-
interests, personal prejudices, sociological influences, political val-

ues, or epistemological presuppositions, is an obvious fiction. In what time zone does it exist? Does it come before or after the cognitive moment? What about the social and political moments? Presumably, they are all secondary, belated, supplementary: first there is language and its law; then there is misreading and its ethical consequences. Evidently, after these come social, psychological, and political matters. Surely, Miller does not believe all this. As people learn to "read," they are already deeply enmeshed in sociopolitical and interpersonal psychological contexts. In addition, the "languages" that people read are themselves social constructs and archives. The presocial, prepsychological, prepolitical moment of linguistic ethical interaction with a text is a fabrication. Significantly, the effect of this fiction is to desocialize, depoliticize, and depersonalize reading. Reading here is an impersonal, apolitical, nonsocial activity—which, however, does have social and personal consequences, but only after the fact. Why does Miller propound this fiction?

One unannounced priority of Miller's project in *The Ethics of Reading* is to save literature from the growing number of liberal and leftist advocates of "discourse" as a social phenomenon or institution. Consider the trajectory of the following intricate passage:

> The ethical moment in reading leads to an act. It enters into the social, institutional, political realms, for example in what the teacher says to the class or in what the critic writes. No doubt the political and the ethical are always intimately intertwined, but an ethical act that is fully determined by political considerations or responsibilities is no longer ethical. It could even in a certain sense be said to be amoral. The same thing could be said of cases in which the apparently ethical is subordinated to the epistemological, to some act of cognition. If there is to be such a thing as an ethical moment in the act of reading, teaching, or writing about literature, it must be sui generis, something individual and particular, itself a source of political or cognitive acts, not subordinated to them. The flow of power must not be all in one direction. There must be an influx of performative power from the linguistic transactions involved in the act of reading into the realms of knowledge, politics, and history. Literature must be in some way a cause and

not merely an effect, if the study of literature is to be other than the relatively trivial study of one of the epiphenomena of society. (4–5)

In this revealing passage, Miller explicitly pits linguistics and ethics against epistemology, sociology, politics, history, and social institutions. Any discipline or mode of understanding that portrays literature as an effect rather than a cause is anathematized. Language and literature cannot be secondary, subordinate phenomena or epiphenomena without being powerless and trivial. In Miller's portrait, the ethical moment of reading must be a primordial and private act, an individual and particularized engagement, a presocial undertaking sui generis; it must beget a flow of power, which engenders social acts and consequences. When *reading* enters the classroom or the journal, it becomes, in Miller's view, *criticism,* that is, a public activity entangled with politics, history, cognition, social institutions, and morals. Reading per se is inaugurating, private, and powerful; criticism is social, public, and comparatively trivial. This entire structure of thought of Miller's is a construction built on a series of "ifs." What motivates Miller here is evidently the widening threat to literature's primacy in the culture as well as the discipline.

It is striking that Miller relies on the classical logic of "cause and effect" to structure his theory of the ethical moment in reading. This logic requires something to precede something; it demands primacy. Wouldn't the "reciprocal interaction" of dialectic make more sense in this situation? Why not say, for instance, that the reading of texts depends on certain linguistic, social, and literary conventions and that the way we learn such codes is through reading? Since language is at the outset and always communal, text is always social text. This is one implication of Saussure's powerful concept of *langue.* However it is construed, reading is a social linguistic transaction, not a private linguistic act. In Miller's hands, literature and criticism undergo privatization and desocialization, but such deracination and mummification preserve them at too high a price. Little would be lost by casting the literary text and its interpretation as social phenomena entangled with linguistics, epistemology, ethics, economics, politics, and history—regimes of reason. To each of these domains or disci-

plines, as much autonomy and specificity as desired can be accorded—
short of elevating one at the expense of all others. The contest of faculties does not require a winner. The deconstruction of primacy
should engender a certain undecidable plurality, which Miller seems
to have forgotten here.

With the emergence in the sixties and thereafter of the black power
movement, feminism, and the New Left and with the contem-
poraneous dissolution of formalist hegemony, certain long-standing
patterns of exclusion came into question. Just as the economic and
political situations of blacks, women, and the poor were vigorously
contested, so too the various strictures in criticism against, for example, reader responses, extrinsic criticisms, and ethicopolitical engagements were effectively called into doubt. For the formalists, criticism's main obligations entailed explication and evaluation of
literary structure and texture. Critics were discouraged from actively
assessing the strengths or weaknesses of thematic materials. Their job
was to respect, admire, and revere aesthetic qualities. Not until the
various challenges to the New Critical paradigm launched in the sixties and later did the practice of irreverent critique slowly start becoming an accepted and respected part of academic literary criticism.
Booth's notion of overstanding and Scholes's special concept of criticism testify to this shift. Evaluation and exegesis are not enough.

Interestingly, the explicit linking of criticism, ethics, and politics
is invariably effected in the social contexts of pedagogy and professionalism. This pattern is figured in the work of Booth and Scholes.
For his part, however, Miller depicts reading as a private, personal
activity, which accounts, in part, for why his version of literary criticism displays a disembodied, fictional quality. For Miller group values and interests are not at stake, as they are for Booth and Scholes,
both of whom are overtly committed to such ethicopolitical goals as
understanding, freedom, and justice. Because he thinks all interpretive reading is unavoidably doomed to become misreading, Miller
emerges as a conservative poststructuralist who believes in the fallen,
imperfectible agency of human being. The unhappy situation of humankind is epitomized by the fall into language, which begets ines-

capable deviance, error, and errancy. For Booth and Scholes misunderstanding can be overcome since it occurs between and among people. For Miller there is no escaping misreading since it afflicts people in their fundamental relation to language. In this context, preoccupation with pedagogy or the professional community evidently makes little sense.

I wish to conclude this discussion by making four general points related to cultural criticism and ethicopolitics. First, it is misleading to characterize criticism as an activity that has distinct ethical and political moments or stages. The relations between ethics, politics, and criticism are too intricate and entangled for this kind of fabricated analytical simplicity. In particular, the complex linkages of any values and interests with ethical, political, social, aesthetic, economic, and theological values and interests need to be posited and explored rather than deemphasized or simplified. Regimes of reason are inescapable as well as useful for cultural analysis. Second, a contemporary criticism that ignores, suppresses, or downplays issues of ethnicity, gender, and class is seriously inadequate given the global situation. Third, while critique in the form of interrogation, resistance, and repudiation has become accepted critical practice in segments of literary academia, it is still too widely regarded as discourteous infringement on poetic and aesthetic values. The old dream of having disinterested, unindoctrinated, "pure" aesthetic exegesis as the preferred mode of criticism survives in many places today, constituting a continuing challenge for the practice of cultural criticism. Fourth, to be programmatic and to reiterate: the work of cultural critique requires unabashed textual and institutional analyses of received values, practices, categories, and representations, a delving into linguistic, epistemological, social, economic, historical, political, ethical, and aesthetic causes, constitutions, and consequences. With cultural matters, one always finds oneself amidst the entanglements of regimes of (un)reason.

2

(De)Authorizing Literary Discourse

The contemporary debates in literary academia concerning the roles and functions of the "author" have, of course, a tangled history that involves a host of disputants, including as main figures Wimsatt and Beardsley, Hirsch, Poulet, Barthes, Foucault, Bloom, Gilbert and Gubar, and as less influential polemicists a broad array of theorists too numerous to list. Rather than providing a conspectus on this contested domain of inquiry, I want to scrutinize the main lines of argumentation in order to propound formulations on literary authorship in line with the enterprise of poststructuralist cultural criticism. In this chapter I shall develop the argument that the "author" is best construed as both a public and private figure, who functions as a relay in regimes of reason, joining literary discourse with social text. As a sociohistorical locus and as a pluralized spokesperson for certain conscious and unconscious interests and values, the "author," in my formulation, opens literary discourse to cultural analysis and critique.

Public and Private Authors

Wimsatt and Beardsley contend that literary discourse exists in the public domain where questions about its genesis engender mere speculation as well as nonliterary historical and psychological inquiry. What a private author personally intended is "neither available nor desirable as a standard for judging the success of a work of literary art"

(3). In order to make this severe protocol applicable to lyric poetry, a genre seemingly fitted to challenge their stance, they employ the compensatory theory of the *persona*—the idea that each lyric poem is the statement of an abstract speaker who is not the author. The general drift toward disembodiment culminates in the following statement: "There is a gross body of life, of sensory and mental experience, which lies behind and in some sense causes every poem, but can never be and need not be known in the verbal and hence intellectual composition which is the poem. For all the objects of our manifold experience, for every unity, there is an action of the mind which cuts off roots, melts away context" (120). The effect of conceiving every literary discourse as severed not only from the author but from the body of life is to render it an autonomous artifact open to "purely" aesthetic analysis and assessment—the goal of formalist analysis.

It is clear that Wimsatt and Beardsley are trying to move literary criticism away from source studies, biographical inquiry, and history of ideas. Their main instrument for this operation is the single-minded application of the genetic fallacy—the common error of confusing a phenomenon and its causes. Disarticulating the literary text from its root systems, they self-consciously situate it in a public arena. Such status and location are gained by denying sociohistorical foundations, causes, and origins. Given the level at which poetic discourse is construed as public, Wimsatt and Beardsley are enabled to avoid psychological, sociological, and historical inquiry. Even the history of literature undergoes exclusion when they limit the reach of allusions—as explicitly in discussing Eliot's *The Waste Land*—to exegetical pertinence and structural integrity within individual texts. Not surprisingly, the genre most challenging to such processes of exclusion, the lyric, is transformed (deformed) into a certain form of drama—the public soliloquy. Had the alteration entailed recasting lyric as epic instead of dramatic, the result would have been to reconnect the spokesperson with the community—an unwanted outcome. The various moves of Wimsatt and Beardsley bring about an ascetical purification and spiritualizing of literary discourse that is zealously distanced from the "gross body of life." We are left with an author who for all practical purposes is dead.

The outcome of Wimsatt and Beardsley's theorizing for criticism can be formulated as an imperative: aesthetic inquiry should have little or nothing to do with psychology, sociology, history, biography, economics, politics, ethics, or any other such "extrinsic" matters. Thus the whole apparatus of literary production, specifically its imbrication in the social formation, is construed as both unreachable and irrelevant. Artistic beauty and pleasure are miraculously freestanding. By programmatically repressing the root systems of literary discourse, such theorizing sets up the return of the repressed, which comes when Wimsatt and Beardsley prescribe what "intrinsic" evidence should properly be used in critical exegesis: "It is discovered through the semantics and syntax of a poem, through our habitual knowledge of the language, through grammars, dictionaries, and all the literature which is the source of dictionaries, in general through all that makes a language and culture" (10). Here the eruption of the intertext, characterized as a cultural repository, signals the unconscious and covert return of the social text. Although linguistic competence is reductively portrayed as a mere adjunct to aesthetic appreciation, it forms the indispensable archival medium of literary production and consumption. Literary creation and literary criticism depend on cultural discourse; regimes of reason are inescapable. Using Saussure's terminology, we can say that Wimsatt and Beardsley unwittingly push *parole* back into *langue,* that is, they deemphasize individually authored speech in favor of unconsciously emphasizing collective discourse pictured as a cultural archive. Literature is public, therefore, not because of the absence of the author but because of the presence of the social text. It is discourse per se that constitutes the body of life of the linguistic community. Aesthetics, therefore, is unavoidably entangled with economics, politics, ethics, history, society. Because it is a cultural construct, enmeshed in communal discourse, literary discourse is not without pertinent origins, interests, and values open to critique as well as exegesis and appreciation. Here we see

that Wimsatt and Beardsley are sometimes right for the wrong reasons: the formalist deauthorization of the author serves to bring back
the social text rather than to hypostatize autonomous literary discourse.

Against Wimsatt and Beardsley and other like-minded formalist
critics, Hirsch argues for the necessity and usefulness of the "author"
in the work of critical understanding. This resurrection of the author
is explicitly conceived and presented as a polemic against critical au-
tonomism, relativism, historicism, individualism, and anarchism;
that is, Hirsch self-consciously offers his work in the broad context of
a conservative cultural politics. For Hirsch, however, the born-again
"author" is not a historical personage knowable through biographical
and psychological inquiry but a logical construction produced by
means of deduction based on principles of probability, appropriate-
ness, and plausibility. Hirsch makes a crucial distinction between the
so-called private and public stances of the "author": "In no sense does
the text represent the author's subjective stance" (241); "the author's
private experiences are irrelevant" (243). Although he shares with
Wimsatt and Beardsley this suspicion of subjective idealism, Hirsch
insists that auctorial "intention" is both relevant and indispensable for
literary interpretation. But "intention" means "awareness" in the phenomenological sense rather than willed purpose or design. To get at
the awareness or "intention" of the (public) author, the critic must
reconstruct the "horizon" of the author, which consists of a unified
and coherent system of expectations, norms, limits, typicalities, and
probabilities common to the writer's culture. Thus the job of interpretation is to extrapolate the "intentional meaning" of the author
within the given contexts of genre constraints and social and literary
conventions, all of which form part of the historical horizon. The endpoint of hermeneutic inquiry is the distillation of probabilistic stable,
determinate, reproducible "intentional" auctorial meaning. In the
case of an anonymous text, the interpreter must posit both a plausible
horizon and a public author.

The concept of the horizon in Hirsch reinstitutes, in part, the body
of life expelled from critical inquiry by the formalists. The horizon,

like the author, is a historical reconstruction that partially brings back regimes of reason by rendering literary discourse a public formation. But this return of the world's body is severely constrained and narrowly construed by Hirsch. To begin with, the crafted horizon must meet strict tests of plausibility predicated on the assumption that the writer's social formation is a coherent, unified system. This is implausible. Any *socius* is likely to have multiple pockets of opposition to the reigning culture. Demonstrably, numerous marginal figures and forces do not enter into Hirsch's horizon. In addition, different strata of culture invariably exhibit unequal stages of development. For instance, in advanced technological capitalist democracies elements of slavery and feudalism exist side by side with aspects of socialism. In the arts today we find vast areas of expression faithfully working with century-old principles of aesthetic realism coexisting with widespread efforts to extend modes of modernist surrealism. The idea of a unified and coherent, relatively homogeneous historical horizon is untenable; it is itself an aestheticized notion based on discredited principles of literary realism. This impoverished historiography disables Hirsch's conceptualization of the horizon. To make the norm, the typical, and the probable the measures of credible historical inquiry is to celebrate unity, uniformity, and regularity and to squelch the abnormal, the marginal, and the disruptive. Too many resisting and oppositional forces are overlooked in this project. The truth is that Hirsch limits the hermeneutic value of the horizon not only by equating it with the hegemonic status quo of "cultural givens," but by rigorously restricting its point of focalization to specific authors. Employing the *langue/parole* opposition, Hirsch declares that "Saussure's distinction nevertheless confirms the critic's right in most cases to regard his text as representing a single *parole*" (233). Thus the language of the community recedes before the author. It is auctorial discourse, not the social text, that preoccupies Hirsch's interpreter. The outcome of such theorizing is to frame the author as both an abstract public persona and a conduit of dominant culture.

Hirsch makes a revealing distinction between "interpretation" and "criticism"—which, in my view, renders his hermeneutical enterprise of limited value to poststructuralist cultural criticism. The purpose of interpretation is to extract auctorial "meaning"—an unchanging, verifiable, reproducible, determinate object. The aim of criticism is to isoiate "significance"—the pertinence, value, and interest for the critic of literary discourse. According to Hirsch, before there can be significance, there must be meaning: the one is added to the other; the one changes over time while the other is constant. In order for the critic to isolate an author's meaning, he must transcend his own interests, values, prejudices, and blind spots. Such abnegation and self-overcoming, prerequisites of interpretation, are dubious hermeneutical fictions. Evidently, the price to be paid for the resurrection of the author is the death of the critic or at least the suspension of the critic's interests (not knowledge) for the duration of the interpretative process. The patent unreality of this scenario compels Hirsch to conceive "interpretation" itself as a two-phased operation: interpretation moves through a prereflective, personal, and emotional stage of identification followed by a reflective, impersonal, and intellectual stage of interpretation proper. "To understand a poem by Keats a reader must imaginatively reenact the doubts, glories, and mysteries which inform Keats' sense of life, but afterwards the reader can subject his imaginative construction to a severe discipline" (x). In other words, the identification and empathy of a practicing critic, conceived here as a private rather than a public figure, precedes and engenders a heroic hermeneutical labor of monkish self-denial. Thus Hirsch's idolatry of textual meanings and of typed authors depends on the unreal temporary bracketing of the critic's horizon. For Hirsch the first and primary task of critical understanding entails the worshipping of hegemonized texts and normalized authors, relegating to secondary, belated, and inferior status the work of evaluation and critique. Such a project promotes, above all, attitudes of quiet attention, respect, forgetfulness, obedience, and self-denial—authoritarian values not befitting cultural literacy in its liberating and enlightening forms.

Among major influential contemporary literary theorists perhaps no one has gone further in revering the "author," humbling the reader, and disarming the critic than Poulet. Where he differs crucially from formalists and hermeneuticists is in his willingness to de-materialize not only the surrounding body of life but the literary "work" and the critic's self. As consciousness of consciousness, criticism for Poulet involves the transportation of the mental universe of the author into the interior spaces of the critic's mind. Such intersub-jectivity focuses on a communion of disembodied minds, engaging the critic in the co-celebration of the "work" (whether single text, oeuvre, or any other discursive segment). Lost in the inner cosmos of auctorial being, the world and eventually the text become unreal for the critic: "Criticism, in order to accompany the mind in this effort of detachment from itself, needs to annihilate, or at least momentarily to forget, the objective elements of the work, and to elevate itself to the apprehension of a subjectivity without objectivity" (68). Such di-vinatory identification with the inner being of the author begets the ideal dissolution of the text and of the reader's self. "Reading, then, is the act in which the subjective principle which I call *I,* is modified in such a way that I no longer have the right, strictly speaking, to con-sider it as my *I*" (57). The consequence for criticism is that all endeav-ors give way completely to divination: "When I read as I ought, i.e., without mental reservation, without any desire to preserve my inde-pendence of judgment, and with the total commitment required of any reader, my comprehension becomes intuitive and any feeling pro-posed to me is immediately assumed by me" (57). The resulting alien-ation and enslavement of the spellbound, possessed reader, enthralled by pure auctorial subjectivity, bear witness to the end of interpreta-tion, evaluation, and critique, all in the interest of bliss in aesthetic awe before the author's spirit. Incredibly, Poulet does not scrutinize the material dialectical dimensions of such unfettered utopianism, that is, he does not inquire into the dynamics of aesthetical forgetful-ness of social history and of self-fashioning.

To Poulet goes the dubious distinction, therefore, of making Hirsch's project seem well-rounded and reasonable. The marriage of minds envisioned by Poulet occurs without regard to authors' or read-ers' horizons: the merging of minds purportedly takes place unhindered by social constraints. Questions of class, gender, race, and justice, for instance, seem unimportant, as do matters of genre, form, style, and structure. The issue of contemporary significance is altogether scrapped by the happily annexed astonished consciousness of the critic whose programmatic subordination approaches abasement. Norms and probabilities are irrelevant here for there is neither a body of life nor cultural givens that shape imaginative utterance.

The antibiographical impulse, the dominant line of contemporary thinking about the author, problematizes the issue of "intention," which in Poulet's case receives scant attention. Whereas Wimsatt and Beardsley scrap "intention" (purpose) and Hirsch recuperates "intention" (awareness), Poulet reconfigures "intention" as pure imagination (spiritual shaping power), which is severed from the chaotic body of social life and personal existence. "The subject who is revealed to me through my reading of it [the work] is not the author, either in the disordered totality of his outer experiences, or in the aggregate, better organized and concentrated totality, which is the one of his writings" (58). The sociohistorical and psychological self of the author dies to give birth to transcendent imagination—a demonic force empowering aesthetic creativity. This ethereal mode of intentionality, if we can call it that, is suprapersonal. What Wimsatt and Beardsley, Hirsch, and Poulet illustrate on the issue of intention is the broad tendency to discredit biographical criticism. In this context it is not surprising that a wide gap has opened between literary theorists and biographers, nor is it a surprise that recent new historicists like Greenblatt have sought to rescue biographical criticism by renewed examination of the complex sociohistorical forces that constitute subjectivity.

Author Functions

Some critics on the left have been quick to condemn Barthes's notorious proclamation of the death of the author, a demise provoked earlier, in various ways, by formalists, hermeneuticists, and phenomenologists. The tendency has been to cast Barthes's version of poststructuralism as a continuation of formalistic modes of thinking.

This is an error, for Barthes's radical cultural politics proclaims specifically the passing of the possessive, privatized, paternal "author" of capitalist culture that has functioned for half a millennium in the Western world.

> The author is a modern figure, a product of our society insofar as, emerging from the Middle Ages with English empiricism, French rationalism and the personal faith of the Reformation, it discovered the prestige of the individual, of, as it is more nobly put, the "human person." It is thus logical that in literature it should be this positivism, the epitome and culmination of capitalist ideology, which has attached the greatest importance to the "person" of the author. . . . The image of literature to be found in ordinary culture is tyrannically centered on the author, his person, his life, his tastes, his passions. (142–43)

> The Author, when believed in, is always conceived of as the past of his own book: book and author stand automatically on a single line divided into a *before* and an *after*. The author is thought to *nourish* the book, which is to say that he exists before it, thinks, suffers, lives for it, is in the same relation of antecedence to his work as a father to his child. (145)

> To give a text an Author is to impose a limit on that text, to furnish it with a final signified, to close the writing. . . . [To refuse the author] liberates what may be called an anti-theological activity, an activity that is truly revolutionary since to refuse to fix meaning is, in the end, to refuse God and his hypostases—reason, science, law. (147)

The effect of Barthes's thinking is to portray bourgeois author-based theory as reactionary ideology respectful of possessive individualism, law, order, authority, meaning, paternity, exclusive ownership, science, and religion. Barthes's whole attack is carried out in the name of liberation, promoting revolution, however vaguely, against modern capitalist society with its culture of celebrity authors and aesthetic commodities. In short, Barthes's anarchistic critique of the author is launched on political grounds—with consequences for critical practices.

Countering the author, Barthes propounds the concept of the scriptor, a functionalist notion providing agency for the emergence of the intertext. "We know now that a text is not a line of words releasing a single 'theological' meaning (the 'message' of the Author-God) but a multi-dimensional space in which a variety of writings, none of them original, blend and clash. The text is a tissue of quotations drawn from innumerable centers of culture" (146). The primary power of the scriptor is to mix writings derived from the archive of culture, conceptualized as a ready-formed unabridged dictionary. A "text is made of multiple writings, drawn from many cultures and entering into mutual relations of dialogue, parody, contestation" (148). The scriptor is a socialized figure because the heterogeneous intertext constitutes his medium: "It is language which speaks, not the author" (143). Without a determining subjectivity or a fixed historical horizon, the scriptor is a polemical replacement for the author of capitalist culture. Models of his scribal activities include the automatic writing, collective authorship, and aleatory texts of tribal bards and surrealist poets. In Barthes's view, the historical institution of authorship covers over and mystifies the scribal, intertextual, anonymous features of writing. To engage in author-centered hermeneutical activities is to participate in reactionary holding operations. As a holding company, ordinary criticism finds it impossible to do without the author. It is worth recalling that Barthes's doctrine of the death of the author is a provocation in the context of a polemic against conservative French academic and journalistic criticism made on behalf of the left-poststructuralist avant-garde associated with *Tel Quel*.

It is not so much Barthes's attack on the "author" that merits criticism from orthodox segments of the left but his accompanying promulgation of the theory of *écriture*, the notion that "writing ceaselessly posits meaning ceaselessly to evaporate it, carrying out a systematic exemption of meaning" (147) and that "*writing* can no longer designate an operation of recording, notation, representation, 'depiction'" (145). The denials of writing's mimetic potentials and its semantic stability evidently disable the critical search for textual meaning and significance, seemingly rendering ideology critique a defunct operation. However, as both *Mythologies* and *S/Z* demonstrate, the semiological notions of mythologizing and of coding recuperate the task of ideological analysis, which is resituated on linguistic grounds where investigations of the discourses of mass media and cultural stereotypes track ideology at work. Despite certain leftist prejudices, poststructuralism is not incompatible with political critique—the work of Foucault and Spivak makes that quite clear, as do various undertakings of Barthes. Aspects of the notion of *écriture* can be harnessed for a project of cultural critique. Ultimately, Barthes's idea of the death of the author begets the birth of the intertext, which connects each text (*écriture*) to social discourses harboring ideological formations open to critique. This constitutes an improvement over the antibiographical theorizing of Wimsatt and Beardsley, Hirsch, and Poulet.

Reacting against certain facets of the enterprise of Barthes and other poststructuralists, Foucault conceives of the "author" in a manner consistent with his broad historiographical project of archeology. In the regimens of social and institutional discourses during particular eras, the "author" comes to occupy specific positions, to follow designated rules, and to serve observable functions. The sociohistorical status, configuration, and value of the "author" can and do change; one can imagine a society in which the production and circulation of discourse would occur in the absence of the concept of authorship. Who can be an author? What roles must she play? How will authorized texts be circulated, valorized, appropriated and by whom? It is questions such as these that direct Foucault's inquiry. While he agrees with others that "in our day literary works are totally dominated by the sovereignty of the author" (126), he goes on to trace this practice back to biblical exegetes who were preoccupied with authenticating (and rejecting) potential canonical sacred texts. Over time the honorific "authorship" came to designate 1) a standard level of quality among texts, 2) a field of thematic coherence, 3) a stylistic uniformity, and 4) a consistency of historical reference. In our society literary discourse possessing the name of an author implies, among a set of texts, relations of homogeneity, filiation, reciprocal interconnection, and authenticity. Moreover, "in our culture, the name of an author is a variable that accompanies only certain texts to the exclusion of others: a private letter may have a signatory, but it does not have an author; a contract can have an underwriter, but not an author; and, similarly, an anonymous poster attached to a wall may have a writer, but he cannot be an author" (124). To conceive an author, then, is to construct a certain significant mode of subjectivity fulfilling designated functions, which need analysis not dismissal. For contemporary critical inquiry the doctrine of the death of the author is, in Foucault's judgment, hasty: "The subject should not be entirely abandoned. It should be reconsidered, not to restore the theme of an originating subject, but to seize its functions, its intervention in discourse, and its system of dependencies" (137). Against those theorists, poststructuralist and otherwise, advocating the deauthorization of literary discourse, Foucault prudently recommends tactical maintenance of the concept of authorship as a means to institutional and ideological analyses of discourse—not reverent biographical reconstruction of either the lives of literary geniuses or the stable meanings of poetic texts.

While Foucault characterizes as ideological the historical individualization of the author and the conferring of certain rights and privileges upon him, he does not embrace the utopian anonymity of the author as promoted by the concept of *écriture.* Here Foucault appears reserved from points of view popularized by Barthes, Derrida, and other poststructuralists. The insightful critique of *écriture* mounted by Foucault casts this mode of the disappearance of the author as, in effect, a subtle preservation insofar as discourse is presented as primordial, creative, sacred, transcendent, requiring commentary and interpretation to ferret out "implicit signification, silent purposes, and obscure contents" (120). The exegetical work of Barthes and Derrida, as in *S/Z* and *Dissemination,* partially bears out Foucault's point. To the extent that *écriture* approaches a universalist theory of discourse, it constitutes a mystification. Curiously, Foucault does not mention the attendant concepts of the intertext and social text, which omission reduces the reach of his polemic. The thoroughgoing linkage of any discourse with its specific cultural archive and regimes of reason is crucial for Foucault. Thus those moments where Barthes, Derrida, and others ignore the historical conditions enabling both discourse and the functions of the individuated subject are, I concur, points of weakness. What Foucault disregards in the concepts of *écriture* and the intertext, however, is their strength in revealing the constituting function of discourse and its imbrication in archival regimes of reason.

"Historical" Authors

To maintain the author as a historical figure is not to guarantee much in particular, as the different projects of Hirsch and Foucault suggest. When we add to this constellation the enterprises of Bloom and of Gilbert and Gubar in rescuing the historical author, we encounter new complications and problems.

What Bloom does is to limit the author's horizon and archive to an extremely slim set of literary texts by grand precursors. Gone are political codes, ethical conventions, economic norms, and social regularities. The whole body of life is reduced to the struggling psyche of the great poet in formation, who grows in power in order ultimately to overcome death and gain immortality. By implication literary discourse consists of a few great works by a few great writers. History amounts to the literary texts of selected geniuses. Criticism entails adulatory diagnostic rhetorical and imagistic analysis of master texts produced by powerful souls anxiously influencing one another. There is no place here for cultural critique; and evaluation takes place before criticism begins its work on the revered canon. Missing is any institutional analysis of the sociohistorical conditions of authorship—of, for example, patronage, book production, distribution mechanisms, reviewing procedures, or readership groupings. All literature is rendered lyrical because "intentionality" is singularly preserved: poetic texts are the compulsive personal expression both of an unconscious drive to triumph over mortality and of a defensive will-to-power over competitors. The death of the author is, therefore, anathema in every sense of the word for Bloom.

Because each strong poet is balefully yet fruitfully influenced by another Promethean poet, the ground of poetry is the literary intertext—construed narrowly in Bloom's theory as a few major texts. Each poem is an "interpoem." High tradition (de)forms the individual talent portrayed by Bloom as an embattled competitive psyche. Such a history of influence amounts to a psychohistory of great men who seek psychologically to defend themselves against enervating poetic father figures and to repress the ravenous wish for immortality. To triumph, the new poet must misconstrue the precursor: misreading is necessary and productive. Strong (inter)poems constitute acts of defensive misreading. Thus Bloom's literary criticism centers itself tyrannically on the psychic selves of grand poets in thrall to precursor poets, who are systematically misread. Since it disregards social history, Bloom's criticism is neither biographical nor historical in the ordinary sense; it is preoccupied with the literary (inter)textual signs of psychopoetic misprisions.

Although he spends almost no time on the matter, Bloom delimits and frames his project in revealing and useful historical ways. He regards his work as dedicated to studying only the great line of Anglo-American poets during the Romantic era, which he dates from 1740 to the present. He is not interested in minor figures nor in other genres. In his view, poetic influence before the Romantic era was salutary; only in recent centuries has it become baleful. Significantly, he does not scrutinize the implications of this historical framing. Nevertheless, he graphically demonstrates the rise of a new mode of subjectivity—the isolated, competitive, threatened, and anxious self of the post-Enlightenment era, which is congruent with the emergence of bourgeois capitalism, the loss of patronage for writers, the commodification of literature through copyright practices, and the marginalization of poetry in particular. Because he is inattentive to the author-function in the emergent social formation of the Romantic era and uninterested in the changing institutional mechanisms of its literary production, Bloom, like others before him, dematerializes literary discourse. What the absence of the sociohistorical horizon and social text permits is a continuation and intensification on Bloom's part of the idea of the author as paternal originating subject who suffers for his great works. For Bloom, since poetry is miraculously free from regimes of reason, cultural critique is inconceivable. Preoccupied with strong male poets, great works, triumph in competition, heroic suffering, and immortality, Bloom's cultural politics is deeply conservative. It is, however, brilliantly revealing in its stark portraiture of the fate of poets in our epoch and suggestive in its account of the deformations enacted in the labors of misreading and of identity formation.

Not surprisingly, Gilbert and Gubar find Bloom at once limited and useful. They contentiously counter his patriarchal concept of the anxiety of influence with their own feminist theory of the "anxiety of authorship," which seeks to account for a developing feminine poetics emergent among Anglo-American women writers in post-Renaissance times. To become an author within the fiercely patriarchal and misogynistic social order requires of a woman writer an arduous passage through silence, alienation, and disease on the way to achieving voice, autonomy, and health by means of reestablishing links with an archetypal Sibyl figure (mother goddess) or female Ur-poet. To create, women authors have to overcome specifically two debilitating cultural roles assigned to them—the angel and the monster. The ennobling precursor poet necessary in the revisionary struggle, portrayed as a mother or sister, summons up a utopian female subculture and tradition of wholeness and power. The battle of the aspiring woman author is against the patriarchal order with its socialization of women into domesticity, selflessness, and inferiority. The precursor provides an example of successful revolt, not of life-threatening competition. From a historical point of view the anxiety of authorship results because women have been "denied the economic, social, and psychological status ordinarily essential to creativity; denied the right, skill, and education to tell their own stories with confidence" (71). The effect of thus assigning an author, however anxious, to a woman's text is to connect the text with the historical plight of women in all its dimensions, economic, social, educational, familial, psychological, political and legal, although Gilbert and Gubar largely limit the scope of their scholarly critique to "literary" matters.

Just as Bloom sketches a grim picture of the historical situation of male poets in the post-Enlightenment epoch, Gilbert and Gubar paint a broad background canvas depicting the destructive subjugation of women in patriarchy. For example, they examine recurring images and themes of illness characteristic of female literary tradition, concluding that "patriarchal socialization literally makes women sick, both physically and mentally" (53). Among women's illnesses traced are agoraphobia, amnesia, anorexia, aphasia, bulimia, claustrophobia, hysteria, and madness in general. Of the ubiquitous madwoman in female literature, they observe "she is usually in some sense the *author's* double, an image of her own anxiety and rage" (78).

Gilbert and Gubar's project is to investigate the rise of the major woman author in recent centuries, focusing on textual details as evidence of psychosocial states of experience endured by women writers. Not infrequently, fictional characters and poetic personae are cast as auctorial projections who reveal existing social ills and anguished states of mind. Methodologically, their mode of feminist psychological literary criticism aims "to describe both the experience that generates metaphor and the metaphor that creates experience" (xiii). Such criticism engages unabashedly in partisan identification with characters, personae, and authors, all of whom become spokespersons on behalf of women. This "epicization" of women's texts is a politico-aesthetic operation based on the premise that "female writing is both revisionary and revolutionary, even when it is produced by writers we usually think of as models of angelic resignation" (80). Women writers are not free to escape their sociohistorical conditions; they are inescapably "trapped in so many ways in the architecture—both the houses and the institutions—of patriarchy" (85). Thus the various methodological wedges often set between texts and "authors" are scrapped: literary discourse is authored; in this case the author is a public figure and spokesperson of a disenfranchised group. Not surprisingly, Gilbert and Gubar exhibit very little concern with biographical scholarship, for the "private author" is not their target. To get at the (public) author one goes through published texts.

For all its insight, the work of Gilbert and Gubar rests on dubious traditional notions of experience, of language, and of representation.

In their account women in earlier times suffered under patriarchal socialization and accurately represented this suffering and this cruel social order in their literary texts. This view is not much different than Wimsatt and Beardsley's idea that there is a gross body of life, of psychological and somatic experience, which lies behind and causes each text. Where formalists, however, decide against examining such material purportedly because of the fictionalizing, distancing, and rhetorical refractions of poetic language, Gilbert and Gubar rush in to retrieve material reality—to describe the experience that generates metaphor. Although they are intermittently aware that language both constitutes "experience" and constructs "reality," they lapse into instrumentalist treatments of discourse and simple mimetic accounts of poetic fictions. Language is a transparent tool of communication between author and reader sending accurate information about the world. None of the contemporary advances made in theories of language and of literary discourse apply here. The result is that the concept of authorship seems mechanistic and retrograde.

Nevertheless, Gilbert and Gubar's psychohistorical theory of the anxiety of authorship and their history of literary anxiety make a significant contribution, opening to view important pockets of resistance within post-Enlightenment regimes of reason. In addition, Gilbert and Gubar detail many sociohistorical and psychological (ir)regularities involved in the constitution of feminine subjectivity—a subjectivity with the power to "intend" beyond the conscious will of the woman writer. Here we see, significantly, that the applications of the dogma concerning the death of the author and the doctrine of the anonymous intertext risk dissolving sociopolitical specificities, undermining the projects of resisting subjects. Foucault's admonition not to abandon the subject bears on this point. But in this matter, Gilbert and Gubar end up championing the rise of the female author in the name of fair play and equal rights: the "author-function" serves to enfranchise women in the republic of letters, not to transform radically the social formation. The struggle of liberal, white, middle-class women against patriarchy is just one of many battles. Poststructuralist cultural critique cannot be limited to

this particular program and its enabling premises and theories—a
point made clear in chapter 5 and elsewhere.

Epical/Epochal Scriptors

In the cultural criticism I am advocating, the "author" is maintained
but framed as a relay in the reticulums of regimes of reason. A main
function of this private-public author is to link individual discourse
with the social text. *Parole* emerges out of *langue*. The author is a scriptor, typically with a name—a specific sociohistorical locus for the intertext. To circumvent the disorders of popular biographical criticism, occupied with reconstructing eccentricities, favorite foods,
and gossip, the private author undergoes an operation of epical and
epochal transcription, emerging as a spokesperson for certain values,
interests, classes, races, groups. Because such an author speaks not
simply for herself but for a specific compact of collective values and
interests, the "intention" of the author is construed at once as willed
purpose, unconscious drive, and epochal utterance. The creation of
discourse is both private and communal event whose production, circulation, and consumption are open to cultural critique.

In my account, the formation of "subjectivity" is a sociolinguistic
and psychohistorical cultural process, involving communities and
networks of institutions (families, churches, schools, courts, hospitals, states). At any given time and place, numerous or few sanctioned
and oppositional subject-positions are available for writers. For male
Romantic poets Bloom charts six subject-positions, whereas for
nineteenth-century woman authors Gilbert and Gubar specify three
(angel, monster, Sibylline prophet). Not surprisingly, each position
entails a code of behavior and implies a particular politics. Such ty-
pologies of literary subject-positions usefully imply a general fluidity
as well as an epochal stability for subjectivity in its resisting and sanctioned modes.

Turning for a moment to the subject-positions of the contemporary
critic, one finds the phenomenon of intuitive identification with the
author to be an especially crucial site of division among theorists.

Where Poulet indulges and then renounces the subjectivity of the critic in the interest of maximum identification with the author, Gilbert and Gubar maximize the subjectivity of the critic in the work of intensifying the sympathetic message of the author. Here identification can lead to self-denial, as in the different cases of Poulet and Hirsch, or to self-extension, as with Gilbert and Gubar. From my point of view it is crucial that identification with the author not be misconstrued as primary or initiatory in the process of critical understanding. Empathy need not precede judgment. From the outset a literary discourse can be pernicious or wrongheaded. I would reverse and render coterminous the dubious sequence "meaning" then "significance": for criticism the negative and positive significances of a discourse shape the construction of its meaning. To conceive of a sequential critical progression from identification to interpretation to critical evaluation is to cast hermeneutical interaction as an unreal distancing progression from inescapable self-indulgent empathy to essential selfless exegesis to optional self-willed assessment. What this model finally advocates is an ascetical purging of the critic's subjectivity in the interest of aesthetic adulation of the author's stance. Explication supplants cultural critique. How a critical theory construes the issue of identification is, therefore, significant because it ultimately involves how the critic's own author-function is situated in relation to regimes of reason. The regimes may be forgotten, repressed, "purged," celebrated, analyzed, or criticized—all such operations go into constituting the subject-position of the critic. On the critic's part I would counsel self-reflection, admitting the limits imposed by the forces of prejudice, the unconscious, and the archive.

None of the most influential contemporary literary theorists on the topic of authorship deals with authorship in relation to cinema, television, advertising, or other popular and mass cultural forms. The major author and the great canon dominate discussions and theories about "literature." But for cultural criticism "literature" is not an immutable ontological category nor an objective entity; rather, it is a variable functional term and sociohistorical formation. "Literature," as Eagleton reminds us, is "a name which people give from time to time for different reasons to certain kinds of writing" (205). Cultural criticism must be able to examine the broad range of discourses in society. As Scholes puts it in *Textual Power,* "We must stop 'teaching literature' and start 'studying texts.' Our rebuilt apparatus must be devoted to textual studies. . . . Our favorite works of literature need not be lost in the new enterprise, but the exclusivity of literature as a category must be discarded. All kinds of texts, visual as well as verbal, polemical as well as seductive, must be taken as the occasions for further textuality. And textual studies must be pushed beyond the discrete boundaries of the page and the book into institutional practices and social structures" (16–17). It is for such tasks that I have constructed my formulation: the "author," a pluralized private-public figure (or figures), is a relay in regimes of reason, connecting individual discourse with the social text and constituting a specific sociohistorical locus for the archival intertext. As the agency, conscious and unconscious, for certain interests, values, and groups, which may well exhibit internal contradictions, the "author" opens local discourse to cultural analysis and critique attentive to institutional factors and ideological matters.

3

Styling ("Poetic") Language, Rhetoric, Discourse

Despite the widespread criticism of Anglo-American formalism following the 1950s, many of its doctrines survive as accepted wisdom and "common sense" for large numbers of literary intellectuals within the academy—a phenomenon perhaps nowhere more evident than with the central issues of ("poetic") language, rhetoric, and discourse. Any critical discussion of language must work through formalist concepts on its way to consideration of recent influential contributions from such theorists as Jakobson, Burke, Lentricchia, White, de Man, Kristeva, Cixous, and Bakhtin. In articulating and promoting the project of poststructuralist cultural criticism, I argue in this chapter against the common practice of ontologizing poetic language as a separate and higher mode of language in favor of a functionalist analysis of literary discourse where "literature" emerges as an interest-laden social category variously defined in different places and times by certain groups with varying outcomes. I characterize literary discourse as at once rhetorical, heteroglot, and intertextual hedged around by institutions and interests, all rendering the referentiality of language perennially problematic and subject to dispute. About discourse I argue that it provides the means for entry into subjectivity, initiating the formation of the unconscious, the differentiation of the body, and the enrollment into regimes of reason. In this light, a paramount task of cultural criticism is discourse analysis committed to inquiry and critique rather than idolatry of "literature."

"Poetic" Language and Literariness

It is, of course, characteristic of Anglo-American formalist thinking
to distinguish sharply between "ordinary" and "poetic" language or
such different uses of language as practical and poetic ones. An early
memorable version of this split occurs in Richards's theorizing about
the difference between the referential or naming function of language
as employed by science and the emotive function of language as manifested in poetry. As Richards presents it, while poetry sometimes refers to things in the world, it typically does not do so: the test of corre-
spondence between words and things is inappropriate to poetic
language, which consists of pseudo-statements. To read literature as
though it referred directly to the world is to commit the referential
fallacy. What most distinguishes poetic language from other modes of
language for Anglo-American formalists is its use of metaphor broadly conceived. On this matter Wimsatt and Brooks declare: "We can
have our universals in the full conceptualized discourse of science and
philosophy. We can have specific detail lavishly in the newspapers and
in records of trials. . . . But it is only in metaphor, and hence it is
par excellence in poetry, that we encounter the most radically and relevantly fused union of the detail and the universal idea" (749). Here
poetic language effects a magical sublation of the concrete and historical with the abstract and universal, of the newspaper and court record
with philosophy and science, all by means of metaphor. About the
ontology of poetry, Ransom proclaims that "there is a miraculism or
supernaturalism in a metaphorical assertion" (139).

The formalist distinctions between ordinary language, scientific
language, and poetic language effectively render poetic language at
once ontologically separate and aesthetically superior. The referentiality of language is not programmatically denied but overcome by
means of rhetoric (that is, metaphor, paradox, ambiguity, and irony).
As Brooks construes it, poetry is unparaphrasable. It does not make
statements and propositions like science, philosophy, law, journalism. Thus to level the special, elite poetic object and to forgo the attendant critical idolatry of aesthetic artifacts is, in Krieger's view, to

renounce tragically the traditional Western appreciation of literature, which purportedly culminates in modern formalism.

The tendency to find poetic language not only linguistically distinctive but spiritually superior is epitomized in much formalistic theory of language. In this regard Wheelwright's celebration of depth language and his critique of steno-language are exemplary. The anti-modern conservative theology motivating this conceptualization of language represents a recurring factor in formalistic modes of thinking whether among New Critics or myth critics (Frye included). Steno-language, the "literal," logical discourse of science, is limited to the public domain of law, necessity, technology, and convention—an arena of denotation and monosignation. Depth language, the translogical, expressive discourse of myth, religion, and poetry, opens into a private realm of freedom and truth—of connotation, paradox, and plurisignation. Where New Critics characteristically prefer poetry to fiction, metaphoricity to literalism, Wheelwright analogously champions myth over allegory, symbolism over didacticism, poetry over science. He further associates realism and mimesis with scientific positivism and logic. Invariably, such spiritualizing formalist theories of poetic language tend to champion certain literary genres (say, metaphysical lyrics over others like realistic serial novels), certain theological notions to secular materialism, certain social values like privacy over collectivity, and certain modes of discourse like poetry and myth to others like science and logic. (The matrix of values here explains why the secular "scientism" of Richards and the collectivist materialism of Kenneth Burke came to vex their formalist contemporaries.) All the considerable talk among formalists of heresies, fallacies, and miracles bears witness to both a religious temperament and a tendency toward purging. The animus against the everyday, the ordinary, the popular, the worldly, the techno-scientific, and the public in the name of poetry testifies to a motivating theologico-aesthetics in search of the numinous and the epiphanic understood to be quickly disappearing from modern life but still miraculously preserved in the metaphorical language of "poetic" texts.

To the extent that some Slavic formalists and structuralists focus on "literariness," their work represents a useful advance over Anglo-American formalists' notions about language. For instance, as I see it, Jakobson's specification of six functions of verbal communication provides some support for the project of (re)framing literary analysis as cultural criticism. (The six include the referential, poetic, phatic, metalingual, emotive, and conative functions.) In his account verbal messages rarely exhibit monopoly of function; the predominance of one function in a hierarchy of others characterizes communication. For example, the poetic function regularly manifests itself not only in poetry but also in political jingles, commercial advertisements, and popular songs. As a result, the study of "poetry" cannot be limited to traditional genres. "Poetry" can show up almost anywhere; the quotidian, the political, the economic, and the aesthetic nestle side by side. Poetry can most broadly be studied in the context of general semiotics rather than poetics or stylistics. In Jakobson's words, "Any attempt to reduce the sphere of the poetic function to poetry or to confine poetry to poetic function would be a delusive over simplification" (69). For instance, to repress the emotive force of lyric poetry or the referential thrust of epic poetry is to reduce their defining richness and heterogeneity. Thus the structuralist concept of literariness, broadly construed, helps us think past literary aestheticism and strict formalism, opening the whole field of social communication to semiotic analysis attentive to matters beyond, but inclusive of, "poeticity."

There are serious limitations to Jakobson's much criticized endeavors. I shall restrict my comments here to several complaints regarding the influential model of six factors of verbal communication (see figure 3.1), which he coordinates with the six functions of verbal communication.

Context

Message

Addresser ———————————————————— Addressee

(Encoder)   (Decoder)

Contact

Code

Figure 3.1

Six Factors of Verbal Communication

Because this mechanistic formulation tends to portray language as instrumental, the hermeneutic labors of decoding are simplified. As messages are sent from one agent to another through a coded medium within a specific social milieu, the successful arrival and decoding of the message seem improbably guaranteed. Neither the medium nor the milieu appear problematical. None of the numerous problems relating to the subject-positions of the author-addresser and the reader-addressee surface in Jakobson's model. In spite of such limitations, the insights that social codes and contexts necessarily shape both the general medium of language and its specific functions constitute an improvement over Anglo-American formalists' representations about the language of poetry.

Rhetoric and Rhetoricity

Like Jakobson, Kenneth Burke facilitates expanding the field of inquiry appropriate to criticism. Characteristically, Burke's vigorous scrutiny of poetic texts leads him toward the "social text" conceived in highly traditional terms as general human experience. "At its best," formalistic close reading, according to Burke, "sustains the intense contemplation of an object to the point where one begins to see not only more deeply into the object but beyond it, in the direction of generalizations about the kinds of art and artistic excellence, and even the principles of human thought and experience universally" (278–79). Burke works through the literary text and aesthetic matters, approaching the social text. In studying symbolic actions, he explicitly links Poetics with Grammar, Rhetoric, and Ethics: Grammar attends to literature as information and knowledge; Rhetoric deals with literature's power in generating responses; Ethics focuses on literature's moral force in constructing personal and social portraits; and Poetics centers on beautiful objects and aesthetic qualities. Whereas Jakobson theorizes a general semiotic framework for critical analysis but restricts his own literary-critical work to relatively limited stylistic inquiry, Burke specifies the narrow tasks of "formalist criticism" but expands his own project to broad cultural analysis. Conceived by Burke as symbolic action, literature leads to analysis in numerous registers: "The greater the range and depth of considerations about which a critic can be explicit, the more he is fulfilling his task as a critic" (272). It is not surprising that Burke's multifaceted project of coordinated interdisciplinary analysis—of "planned incongruity" attentive to anthropology and psychology, sociology and geography, politics and ethics, religion and aesthetics—struck early formalists as a mongrelizing operation and later cultural critics as a heartening precursor. Among prominent contemporary cultural critics, Burke has many admirers, particularly Lentricchia and White, both of whose formulations on rhetoric expand upon the master in productive ways.

Inspired by Burke, Lentricchia's project of "rhetoric" construes the creation, circulation, and consumption of cultural discourse as constituting the primary moving force in the institution, maintenance, and perpetuation of society and its ruling interests. Lentricchia's premise is that the substance of ideology is "revealed to us *textually* and therefore must be grasped (read) and attacked (re-read, rewritten) in that dimension" (42). The hegemonic and counterhegemonic work of culture takes place in language; the agency of social action and change is rhetoric. The main task of academic cultural criticism, therefore, requires oppositional rhetorical analysis and its application in pedagogical arenas.

Regarding "literature," Lentricchia, like Williams, laments the progressive shrinking of its definition from Renaissance times as the whole body of books and writings to Romantic and modern times as imaginative writing narrowly conceived. "Literature" in its current sense has attained its dubious identity and distinction "by attempting to empty itself of historical, scientific, and generally utilitarian value" (123). (In this endeavor, the theorizing of New Critics is particularly culpable.) Countering this purified and puerile poetics requires redefinition: "The literary is never only the elite canon of great books; it is also what we call 'minor' literature and 'popular' literature. But it is more even than what this expanded definition would allow. It is all writing considered as social practice. . . . The literary is all around us, and it is always doing its work upon us" (157). Self-consciously and polemically, Lentricchia equates "literature" with social discourse understood as embodying ideological and counterideological elements and forces, connecting the "literary" with social reality, history, and especially power. As persuasive praxis, literature is rhetoric.

To establish an oppositional project of critique, Lentricchia takes recourse in political realism and an attendant view of language as willed action. It is not surprising, then, that he singles out for special attack de Man's theory of language, characterizing it as an enervating obfuscation that hinders textual analysis from reaching the "realities" of power, ideology, and hegemony. In Lentricchia's thinking, to the extent that literary theory portrays language as opaque, noncommunicative, or noninstrumental, language is aestheticized and cut off from the social text. But from a poststructuralist point of view Lentricchia fosters a premature closure of the play of the signifier, that is, he encourages an instrumentalizing theory of language that simplifies linguistic duplicity and heteroglossia, and he risks scrapping the distinctive categories of the poetic and the aesthetic. This represents less a tactical expansion and redefinition of "literature" than its reduction and demise.

What Lentricchia helps me to extrapolate is a concept of "literature" as a contentless ideological category which in certain times and places is activated and substantiated in particular ways for specific reasons. At most there is a "literature function." In relation to any one regime of reason, the "literature function" works in certain ways fulfilling particular tasks and abetting specific interests. In this connection present-day leftist and liberal critiques of "literature" should be construed as attacks not on the ontology of the presumed true poetic text but on the whole way "literature" is today defined and utilized. If I now (re)define "literature" as all writing, I am, in part, asking that the kind of intellectual respect and careful attention normally accorded literature be given to discourse in general. Typically, such a call attacks elitism in the name of democratization, particularly in seeking to show the reigning canon of so-called great literature as a sexist, racist, and classist construction. Here a self-conscious return is staged of all that has been purged from "literature" especially by precursor formalists. The battle over the definition of "literature" involves politics as well as aesthetics, framing rhetoric as both persuasive and figurative.

While Lentricchia extends Burke's insights about the persuasive power of rhetoric, White makes use of Burke's formulations on the four master tropes. White's structuralist project of metahistory presents modern historical discourse as at once inescapably aesthetic, ethicopolitical, epistemological, and tropological. As narrative, history writing favors particular modes of emplotment (either romance, tragedy, comedy, or satire). Each such literary form exhibits an affinity for a particular mode of ideology, including, respectively, anarchism, radicalism, conservatism, and liberalism. Homologous with these kinds of plot and politics are specific forms of argumentation or deduction, namely so-called formist, mechanistic, organicist, and contextualist methods. Using Burke's tropological theory of language, White ultimately grounds the four structural sets of emplotment, ideology, and argument in rhetoric. To be able to narrate, value, and explain historical data, White argues, a historian must constitute the field as an object of thought: this generative act of prefiguration is tropological—with metaphor, metonymy, synecdoche, and irony serving as the four preconscious master figures of thought. According to White, "Thought remains the captive of the linguistic modes in which it seeks to grasp the outline of objects inhabiting its field of perception" (xi). In this formulation, White renders the unconscious patterns of figuration the determinants of epistemology, ethicopolitics, and aesthetics. Rhetoric becomes a fundamental discipline. Along the way, however, White implies that rhetorical language is both foundational and prior to all else—a faulty notion common to certain kinds of (post)structuralist theorizing which I examined and criticized when discussing Scholes and Miller in chapter 1, where I explicitly argue against framing ethicopolitics as epiphenomenal with language as ground.

For contemporary literary theorists the decisive intervention in the debate over rhetoric comes with de Man's declarations about "rhetoricity." De Man starts out preoccupied with Nietzsche's observation that tropes are not added to or subtracted at will from language because they constitute its very nature. In *Allegories of Reading* de Man states, "The straightforward affirmation that the paradigmatic structure of language is rhetorical rather than representational or expressive of a referential, proper meaning . . . marks a full reversal of the established priorities which traditionally root the authority of language in its adequation to an extralinguistic referent or meaning, rather than in the intralinguistic resources of figures" (106). Language emerges as always, at once and originarily, figural or rhetorical rather than referential or representational. No primordial unrhetorical language exists. As the distinctive feature of language, rhetoricity necessarily undermines truth and opens up "vertiginous possibilities of referential aberration" (10). Here de Man subverts traditional notions of referentiality, radically deinstrumentalizing language and seemingly exceeding the New Critic's hedgings on linguistic reference. As a determining force, rhetorical language for de Man engenders man and the world, constituting something like a (prison)house of being with nowhere any foundations or origins outside duplicitous language. From the point of view of traditional poetics, this concept of language renders especially dubious mimetic and expressive accounts of literature. It dramatically broadens the idea of the referential fallacy, promoted by New Critics, to include language in general, not simply poetic language. Significantly, however, de Man retains the category "literature," labeling "literary" any densely rhetorical texts whether they are poetic (metrical), philosophical, political, or critical works. (This is reminiscent of Jakobson's tactic with poeticity.) In *Blindness and Insight* de Man declares that "the criterion of literary specificity does not depend on the greater or lesser discursiveness of the mode but on the degree of consistent 'rhetoricity' of the language" (137*n*). In a similar formulation, de Man reaches "the conclusion that the determining characteristic of literary language is indeed figurality, in the somewhat wider sense of rhetoricity" (285). In sum, all language is inherently rhetorical, only "literary" language is characteristically more so wherever it happens to appear.

Although White depicts rhetoric as foundational, he curtails disabling aberrations and duplicities by designating four specific master tropes structurally aligned with particular modes of deduction, ideology, and narration. Unlike de Man, White's theory of rhetoric operates in a structuralist project dedicated to carefully delimiting and typologizing the decisive ethicopolitical, generic, and argumentative forms employed in history writing. The effect of de Man's poststructuralist theorizing is to render ethicopolitical, generic, and epistemological matters radically undecidable. The resultant critical posture more or less defers all considerations except puzzling over sliding figures in the labors of reading. Lentricchia's notion that language does the persuasive work of ideology and requires from critics oppositional rhetorical scrutiny is incompatible with de Man's thinking because it rushes over the permanently problematical gaps opened by the figural oscillations characteristic of language, especially "literary" language. Whereas for Lentricchia rhetoric has to do with the persuasiveness of language and its active involvements with power and ideology, rhetoric, for de Man, designates, first and foremost, the unreadable figurality of language and its (de)constructions of cognition. Politics is a secondary consideration or, more accurately, politics attends rhetoric, being subject to its disruptive sways and performative oscillations.

It is significant that, despite his conception of allegory as prefiguring a prior text, de Man rarely acknowledges intertextuality or the social text. Among leading first-generation poststructuralists he is alone in this regard. Ostensibly, his encounters with "grammar" forestall moving beyond the local debilitating aberrations of rhetoricity. With poststructuralists it is common for the social text to infiltrate "cultural texts," usually by means of such forces as intertextual sedimentations and generic codes, etymological root systems and logocentric conventions, archival discursive regularities and traces of precursor figures. Rarely are the sociohistorical dimensions of language, rhetoric, and discourse denied; if anything, they are exhibited as evidence, alternately and problematically, of heterogeneity, univocity, arbitrariness, regularity, and contradiction. One thinks here of Barthes's handling of the five codes in *S/Z,* of Derrida's tracking of traditional philosophical binaries in *Of Grammatology,* of Kristeva's theorizing of the genotext and phenotext in *Revolution in Poetic Language,* of Foucault's specifying of panoptical regimens in *Discipline and Punish,* of Bloom's charting of epochal influences in *A Map of Misreading,* of Lyotard's renderings of metanarratives in *The Postmodern Condition*, and of Deleuze and Guattari's outlinings of molar formations in *Anti-Oedipus.*

To understand de Man's theory of rhetoric, one should attend to his observations about grammar in *Allegories of Reading*. In his view, "To distinguish the epistemology of grammar from the epistemology of rhetoric is a redoubtable task" (7). Grammar interrupts the vexing relation of rhetoric to reference, creating the very possibility of figurality and exacerbating the aberrations of referential meaning. The impersonal machine-like force of "grammar generates texts only in the absence of referential meaning" (269). Grammar is a motor that unconsciously produces sentences unaware of and indifferent to meaning. Powered by grammar, the referential oscillations of figural rhetoric emerge doubly unreadable. Perennial questions about intention and will become nostalgic in this scenario. To make a text yield meaning requires arbitrarily stabilizing rhetorical aberrations and thereby shutting down grammatical play. In this operation de Man does not deny the ordinary phenomena of linguistic reference, meaning, and persuasion; he renders them, however, both secondary and problematic by casting the performativity of grammar and rhetoric as the groundless "ground" of language, especially "literary" language.

In the chapter I have been quoting from, titled "Promises," de Man deconstructs Rousseau's *Social Contract,* revealing fragmentations within monadic metaphorical totalities, which, in this case, are political concepts, especially notions of land ownership, political representation, social contract, and the legality of the state. About his analytical labor de Man flatly states: "We are not here concerned with the technically political significance of this text, still less with an evaluation of the political and ethical praxis that can be derived from it. Our reading merely tries to define the rhetorical patterns that organize the distribution and the movement of key terms—while contending that questions of valorization can be relevantly considered only after the rhetorical status of the text has been clarified" (258). It is clear that de Man privileges formalistic rhetorical analysis in a philological mode: he seeks to track the (dis)articulation of key terms amidst large figural patterns. The general outcome of the analysis, however, is to undermine the political concepts framing the theory of social contract. Yet markedly, de Man insists that questions of reading precede matters of ethicopolitical theory or praxis. More pointedly, de Man, here as elsewhere, explicitly avoids "questions of valorization" with the consequence that the results of his analysis for political theory and practice remain studiously unexamined.

Reading between the lines, one could extrapolate something like a textual politics of de Man: his celebrations of atomizations and his criticisms of totalizations suggest an eccentric mode of libertarianism. Here he appears dubious about ideas of ownership and property, of political representation and the state, and especially of harmonious collectivities. Because such a "politics" is heterogeneous, it cannot be situated simply on the typical left-to-right spectrum. It seems part neoconservatism and part anarchism.

Both de Man's commitment to rhetorical analysis and his refusal of ethicopolitical valorization characterize a certain brand of formalistic poststructuralism. What is most obviously troubling with this mode of theorizing is the notion that rhetorical analysis can and should precede all else. The idea that a critic can encounter a text limiting the encounter on all fronts to a grammatico-rhetorical inquiry is highly questionable, if only because it rests on a dubious hierarchical base/superstructure model where language is the "ground" of ethics, politics, and epistemology, which are belated, secondary, and epiphenomenal. In my account, language, as it operates, simultaneously unleashes grammatical, figural, epistemological, and ethicopolitical forces and effects with no way of assigning priority to these outcomes. To put grammar and rhetoric before epistemology, ethics, and politics is to state a preference as a truth, and this metaphysical preference works to set unreal boundaries between language, knowledge, and power—with the result that critical inquiry remains permanently preoccupied with textual exegesis and stalled at the threshold of cultural analysis and critique.

The Body, the Unconscious, and the Social Order

Significantly, theories of poetic language and rhetoric regularly omit considerations of physiology, psychosexuality, and sociality. In this

area the early work of Kristeva and that of Cixous is particularly helpful in opening language theory to crucial concerns of cultural analysis.

In her difficult Lacanian distinctions between the "semiotic" and
the "symbolic" domains and the "genotext" and "phenotext," Kristeva
usefully theorizes routes between the subject and the social formation,
the (pre)linguistic order and the social text. The "semiotic" for
Kristeva designates the disposition within the body of instinctual
drives as they affect language. During the mirror stage of human development, the time when subject/object breaches occur and consciousness arises forming the unconscious, language emerges, allow-
ing entry into the domain of rules (grammar, law, paternal
functioning, social constraints). This "symbolic" realm follows upon
the "semiotic." Using the heterogeneous realms of the semiotic and
the symbolic, Kristeva articulates a general theory of text:

> What we shall call a *genotext* will include semiotic processes but also
> the advent of the symbolic. The former includes drives, their dis-
> position and their division of the body, plus the ecological and so-
> cial system surrounding the body, such as objects and pre-Oedipal
> relations with parents. The latter encompasses the emergence of
> object and subject, and the constitution of nuclei of meaning in-
> volving categories. . . . Designating the genotext in a text re-
> quires pointing out the transfers of drive energy that can be de-
> tected in phonematic devices (such as the accumulation and
> repetition of phonemes or rhyme) and melodic devices (such as in-
> tonation or rhythm), in the way semantic and categorical fields are
> set out in syntactic and logical features. (86)

The genotext can thus be seen as language's underlying foundation.
We shall use the term *phenotext* to denote language that serves to
communicate, which linguistics describes in terms of "competence" and "performance." The phenotext is constantly split up and
divided, and is irreducible to the semiotic process that works
through the genotext. The phenotext is a structure (which can be
generated, in generative grammar's sense); it obeys rules of communication and presupposes a subject of enunciation and an ad-

dressee. The genotext, on the other hand, is a process; it moves through zones that have relative and transitory borders and constitute a *path* that is not restricted to the two poles of univocal information between two fully fledged subjects. (87)

What is especially helpful here is the theory of the genotext because it conceptualizes facets of discourse often overlooked. The phenotext names, like Jakobson's model, the communicative dimensions of language. However, this mode of discourse obscures the attendant bodily aspects of language, as manifested in rhythm, syntax, and other "preconscious" marks like sound symbolism and rhyme. The imbrication of the genotext within the ecological and social orders and, further, its genesis within the body and its drives have the effect of socializing and materializing both the unconscious and the body from which language inescapably stems. All signifying processes, in Kristeva's view, include both the genotext and the phenotext, though certain modes of phenotext curtail the genotext, just as certain kinds of genotext, particularly avant-garde modernist texts, evade the full force of the phenotext. There is never pure phenotext or genotext; all texts partake of the symbolic and the semiotic.

Where Anglo-American formalists insightfully portray poetic language as an approximating evasion of the phenotext, they badly mischaracterize the poetic genotext by forgetting the body, the unconscious, and the wider social-ecological contexts. Jakobson runs similar risks. Against the formalists Burke's followers retrieve the unconscious and the social order, but not the bodily drives—a telling omission. In addition, Lentricchia and White politicize the text in a broad way that Kristeva doesn't. Here I find Kristeva at fault for narrowly defining "politics" as that which is disruptive and radical.

According to Kristeva, the modernist genotext "has a tendency to dispense with political and social signifieds. It has only been in very recent years or in revolutionary periods that signifying practice has inscribed within the phenotext the plural, heterogeneous and contradictory processes of signification encompassing the flow of drives, material discontinuity, political struggle and the pulverization of language" (88). What Kristeva does is to historicize (only) a radical politics in her poetic theory—purportedly most texts do not manifest the "political" dimension of the semiotic; only some special few revolutionary and postmodernist texts do. The inscription of "politics" in the text is never guaranteed. Just as Wheelwright's binary distinction between steno-language and depth language serves to valorize depth language, so Kristeva's binary differentiation of phenotext and genotext works to privilege genotext. However, where Wheelwright champions mythology, religion, and aesthetics, Kristeva celebrates the flows of desire and bodily rhythms in "revolutionary" literature and art. Although she doesn't denigrate the quotidian, she does end up privileging the avant-garde genotext, which seems a needless maintenance of elitist modernist aesthetics.

If we contrast de Man's notions about language with Kristeva's, we turn up several telling insights about the former's limitations. With de Man the generative forces of textuality are grammar and rhetoric with no linkages to the body, the unconscious, and the social order. Predictably, de Man displays no abiding interest in psychoanalysis, sociology, or political theory. His mode of reading appears, consequently, obsessive and puritanical. Questions of gender, race, and class receive no emphasis, nor do matters pertaining to rhythm and sound often gain attention. The symbolic (mis)representations within the social order, the (mis)constructions of the body-self, the (counter)forces of will, power, ideology, and praxis, the (de)formations enforced by institutions—all such concerns wait at the threshold of grammar/rhetoric, the space where phenomena come into undecidable being. Of course, certain followers of de Man like Felman and Johnson have reemployed his categories and tactics with overt psychoanalytical and political interests in their work of cultural analysis. The mode of analytical atomization developed by de Man can be used to deconstruct, demystify, and delegitimate questionable educational theories, political practices, institutional regimens, and social arrangements. But de Man himself permanently defers cultural critique.

Because it has special value for cultural criticism, Cixous's utopian theory of *écriture féminine,* like Kristeva's concepts of the semiotic and the symbolic, warrants discussion here. In Kristeva's view the entry into the symbolic order initiates the separation of the emergent self and the (m)other, the acquisition of language, the formation of the unconscious, and the enrollment into the patriarchal social order, all instigating processes of loss, alienation, and desire. According to Cixous, a presymbolic, mother-centered, nonsubjugated space of bodily drives can and should be explored in a new feminine writing: "Women must write through their bodies; they must invent the impregnable language that will wreck partitions, classes, and rhetorics, regulations and codes" (256). *Écriture féminine* is explicitly conceived in opposition to patriarchal grammar, syntax, and rhetoric, and it is presented as a politico-aesthetics seeking to bring about revolutionary cultural change. "A feminine text cannot fail to be more than subversive. It is volcanic; as it is written it brings about an upheaval of the old property crust, carrier of masculine investments; there's no other way. There's no room for her if she's not a he. If she's a her-she, it's in order to smash everything, to shatter the framework of institutions, to blow up the law, to break up the 'truth' with laughter" (258).

The theory of *écriture féminine* has problems as well as strengths. It ontologizes and essentializes "woman," linking her firmly with the unconscious, the body, the mother, the presymbolic—the very imprisoning spaces constructed by the patriarchy. Since "feminine writing" is admittedly written by men like Genet and Joyce as well as by women like Colette and Duras, it is not actually a "feminist" practice; it celebrates the avant-garde above other writing. While the theory of *écriture féminine* seeks to respect and to multiply differences, it frequently ends up declaiming in the singular for the "new woman" and feminine writing—not women and writings. What the doctrine of *écriture féminine* contributes to poststructural cultural criticism, despite its problems, are crucial concepts of the body and the unconscious as genderized (socialized and politicized), of writing as both a site of struggle and a utopian arena for social transformation, of language as the producer of differences and of subjectivities, and of grammar and rhetoric as ideological mechanisms (contra de Man).

Heteroglot Discourse and Poetry

Shortly before his death Raymond Williams had occasion to reflect upon the development of cultural study in recent decades, and he singled out the advances made by the Bakhtin circle in the area of language theory. Cultural critics today regularly invoke Bakhtin, relying on his critiques of formalism and stylistics and employing his theory of discourse, especially the general notion of "heteroglossia." Here is Bakhtin:

> At any given moment of its evolution, language is stratified not only into linguistic dialects in the strict sense of the word (according to formal linguistic markers, especially phonetic), but also—and for us this is the central point—into languages that are socio-ideological: languages of social groups, "professional" and "generic" languages, languages of generations and so forth. From this point of view, literary language itself is only one of these heteroglot languages—and in its turn is also stratified into languages (generic, period-bound and others). And this stratification and heteroglossia, once realized, is not only a static invariant of linguistic life, but also what insures its dynamics: stratification and heteroglossia widen and deepen as long as language is alive and developing. Alongside the centripetal forces, the centrifugal forces of language carry on their uninterrupted work; alongside verbal-ideological centralization and unification, the uninterrupted processes of decentralization and disunification go forward.
>
> Every concrete utterance of a speaking subject serves as a point where centrifugal as well as centripetal forces are brought to bear. The processes of centralization and decentralization, of unification and disunification, intersect in the utterance; the utterance not only answers the requirements of its own language as an individualized embodiment of a speech act, but it answers the requirements of heteroglossia as well; it is in fact an active participant in such speech diversity. (271–72)

For cultural criticism there are five important contributions here. First, language is conceived as utterances of speaking subjects, that is, it is presented as "discourse" (not impersonal, prevocal signifiers, tropes, grammar, etc.). Second, discursive language is characterized by centrifugal forces of stratification, including the formations of distinct dialects, different speech genres, and special group languages (age groups, professional groups, class groups, etc.). Third, the contending linguistic strata typical of language are cast explicitly as socio-ideological phenomena. Fourth, "literary language" is portrayed as only one of many strata, which itself is divided by generic, stylistic, and other distinctive markers. And fifth, the discourse of the individual is framed by the discourse of the society, meaning all discourse participates inescapably in heteroglossia. The effect of such concepts is to conceive literature as a segment of social discourse stratified into numerous contending ideological dimensions: the text is part of the social text, an arena of struggle.

For Bakhtin, the novel is the most heteroglot and poetry the least heteroglot among literary types. Not surprisingly, he prefers the novel. There are problems with this line of thought. "Diversity of voices and heteroglossia enter the novel and organize themselves within it into a structured artistic system. This constitutes the distinguishing feature of the novel as a genre" (300). On the other hand, "the language of poetic genres, when they approach their stylistic limit, often becomes authoritarian, dogmatic, and conservative, sealing it off from the influence of extraliterary social dialects" (287). Bakhtin associates the discourse of poetry with artificiality, standardization, monologization, centralization, unification, and centripetal force. Furthermore, "rhythm," in his view, "serves to strengthen and concentrate even further the unity and hermetic quality of the surface of poetic style, and of the unitary language that this style posits" (298). He notes, however, that low poetic genres, especially satiric and comic forms, exhibit latitude for heteroglossia.

Whereas poetry is pushed toward the margins, "rhetoric" is nudged toward the social center by Bakhtin. Conceived as audience-oriented persuasive speech, rhetoric—manifested in political utterances, journalistic writings, and didactic discourses—engages in dialogue and struggle, being a near neighbor of the novel. The poetry that Bakhtin admires is both novelistic and rhetorical as, for example, Mennippean satire.

What the peculiar genre preferences of Bakhtin reveal are a troubling value system and point of view situating literary discourse on a spectrum that ranges from positive polylogue to negative monologue—from the heterogeneous social collective to a unified ruling authority—with the heteroglot novel at the good extreme and the hermetic poem at the bad extreme. To me this spectrum makes little sense. To counter it, I would "novelize" poetry using "literary" intertexts and regimes of reason. Specifically, I would link the languages of poems with literary traditions, complex etymologies, conventions of grammar and syntax, stereotypical figures and images, historical discursive regularities, reigning and subaltern "dialects," prosodic systems, patterns of dominant and subordinate communicative functioning, gender, race, and class markers, and "symbolic" and "semiotic" features. I would locate poems in the interstices of enabling institutions, including printers, publishers, and book vendors as well as agencies of literacy like churches, schools, and libraries. I would show poems as the statements and fantasies of interested spokespersons who promote, both consciously and unconsciously, certain beliefs, representations, categories, and principles, and who repress other such specifiable values. This task involves socializing and materializing "hermetic poems" and doing so by setting them amid the intertextual networks and grids of regimes of reason. As I conceive it, hermetic poems are heteroglot formations.

Here I find suggestive the observations of Stephen Henderson, offered in the preface to his collection of *poems* by African-American writers in the context of the black aesthetic movement of the 1960s. American black English is a politicized language linked with a two-hundred-year-old history of slavery and oppression. To conceptualize the distinctiveness of this black culture, Henderson theorizes a cultural unconscious, a "Soul-Field," which is a historically formed repository of social experiences, religious practices, and collective aspirations. Out of this archive emerges black expression which is steeped in "soul." To specify the distinct structural and thematic features of American black poetry, Henderson isolates ten traits of black speech and ten traits of black music, covering special modes of folk and formal rhyme, allusion, diction, imagery, rhythm, tone, character, and genre, all of which shape and characterize African-American poetic expression. "Literature," as Henderson puts it, "is the verbal organization of experience into beautiful forms, but what is meant by 'beautiful' and by 'forms' is to a significant degree dependent upon a people's way of life, their needs, their aspirations, their history—in short, their culture" (4). What constitutes aesthetic beauty and poetic form is neither necessarily nor factually the same for African Americans and Euro-Americans. As the ground of expression, cultural histories and forms infiltrate aesthetic phenomena. In Henderson's account, poetry is specifically not sealed off from the body of collective experience. Quite the contrary, though such "experience" appears perhaps too homogeneous here. (I shall have more to say about black aesthetics in chapter 5.)

I want to postulate some axioms specifically about "poetry" for poststructuralist cultural criticism. The more hermetic a poem appears, the more it reveals the scope of (repressed) heteroglossia. Linguistic defamiliarization and stylistic estrangement constitute not simple avant-garde alienation from the social body but intricate efforts to attract and awaken the community by reshaping its discourse. Poeticity, however apparently pure or hermetic, is variously and complexly coded, partaking in regimes of reason. There is no outside of the social text. Heteroglossia characterizes literary languages, poetic as well as novelistic, lyric as well as dramatic and epic. To regard poetry as a special form of unparaphrasable pseudo-statement is both to mummify poetry and to depoeticize discourse in general.

Among the advantages for cultural criticism of conceiving language as heteroglot *discourse* are, in my view, its linkages with interested subjects, its location in the public spaces of society, its foregroundings of differences and struggles among subjects and groups, and its stratifications into segments, dialects, jargons, genres, and minority tongues. By grafting a broad notion of intertextuality onto this concept of discourse, we can enrich the theory of language by adding as aspects of discourse the stratifying forces of etymology, grammar, syntax, and figurality, as well as conventions of rhythm, imagery, characterization, representation, plot, and theme. In addition, we can take into account, mindful of Foucault's work, the dispositions of discourses amid bodies enabled and constrained by grids of institutions, as, for example, families, schools, churches, workplaces, hospitals, courts, state agencies, and media. Given such a view, we can theorize "literature" as a social category of discourse variously defined in different places and different times with varying interests and outcomes. There is no ontology of literature; there are only literature functions—functions in relation to specific languages, intertexts, institutions, regimes of reason.

Aberrant Subjects

The battles in contemporary societies waged by minorities over such issues as fair employment and wage practices, equal educational and housing opportunities, and an end to discriminatory practices in courtrooms, media headquarters, and government agencies extend to literature classrooms, libraries, and research granting foundations. In recovering the literatures of women, African Americans, "black" Britons, immigrant Asians, native Americans, working-class writers, gays, and other suppressed groups, we inevitably engage in reconceptualizations of and struggles over language, literature, literary research, and pedagogy. Given this context, the formulation of literary discourse as heteroglot and intertextual hedged around by institutions and interests holds obvious attractions, offering a poetics and suggesting a hermeneutics suited to the enterprise of cultural criticism.

The cultural inquiry being recommended here can put to good use the atomizing tendencies advocated by poststructuralism. The concept of language as stratified heteroglot discourse is a case in point. "Language" here breaks into a hodgepodge of overlapping and contending languages. Literature turns into a modulated functionalist notion of "literatures." Crucial in the poststructuralist critique of totalization is the attendant critique of hierarchization. No language or literature is inherently or ontologically better than any other. The elevation of certain modes and genres of discourse happens at the expense of others. The exclusion of the others, typically a violent operation, requires inquiry, critique, and revaluation.

In this light, the issue of linguistic truth needs comment. The performativity of languages makes the issue of referentiality perennially problematic for all modes of discourse, political as well as literary, economic as well as religious, educational as well as legal, however simple or complex. As a pragmatic matter, disputes regarding questions of referentiality are inescapable and essential. Consider the sentence "Americans are a free people." What is the referential status of this utterance? Do we get different answers if we take it as a political, economic, legal, or historical statement? Does the speaker make a difference? What about the audience? A markedly trivial instance of discourse, as in "the White House is white," suggests that adjudication is often but not always necessary. Even so, the "whiteness" of the White House can be variously construed to designate paint color, moral status, racial bias, historical accident, lack of imagination, etc. Here again an appropriate critical axiom is—referentiality is negotiable, a point discussed further in chapter 6. In any case, monosignation is a construct, and linguistic errancy is more nearly the norm. But however aberrant referentiality may be, it comes down to cases for purposes of cultural inquiry and such cases engender critical disputes on the way to "resolutions."

In styling language as heteroglot discourse, I have retained the "speaking subject." This subject has/is a body and an unconscious, which are differentiated during entry into the symbolic realm of family relations, social conventions, historical regularities, patriarchal patterns, and cultural codes. Situated at specifiable intersections of regimes of reason, the socialized subject, however divided and in process, serves as a spokesperson employing already used discourse whose grammar, figurality, and rhythm condition both subjectivity and speech acts. Grammar, rhetoricity, and rhythm can be manipulated but not ultimately extinguished because their preconscious and constituting collective aspects put them, in part, beyond conscious individual control. Language speaks (wo)man just as (wo)man speaks language. To the extent that consciousness is linguistic, language is determining and inescapable—even if the subject is silent. Among literatures is the literature of sign language. The point is the theory of discourse being propounded here is not phonocentric: it aims not to privilege voice over writing, sound over silence, consciousness over the unconscious, interiority over exteriority, referent over signifier, presence over absence. As the means for entry into both subjectivity and the symbolic domain, discourse is, at once and indissolubly, social and "transcendental." *Archi-écriture* and heteroglot utterance are equiprimordial in the formation of the social subject, meaning language as a constituting force shapes subjectivity and social subjects as shapers of language contour discourse and subjectivity—with no way of deciding ontological priority.

4

(De)Coding (Generic) Discourse

Literary and critical theory, from Aristotle and Horace to Frye and Todorov, are perennially preoccupied with the kinds and forms of literature. Thinking in this domain is fraught with complications and interesting possibilities. Significantly, contemporary struggles over genre theory are often displaced, surfacing indirectly in battles over the canon, the literature syllabus and core curriculum, and the status of hybrid and "nonliterary" forms. Because genre theory remains central to much contemporary literary criticism and pedagogy, its understanding is important for a poststructuralist cultural criticism seeking a broader base within the contentious realm of academic literary analysis. To get at the issues involved and to intervene productively in this area of inquiry, I want to open to critical scrutiny the theories of genre propounded by Wellek and Warren, Frye, Todorov, and Rosmarin. And since I find Lyotard's observations on the "genres of discourse" suggestive, though not related strictly to literary matters, I wish to extend his insights toward a poststructuralist conceptualization of genre. Finally, because positions taken by feminists on the connections between gender and genre are significant and useful, I shall single out some key issues as essential to formulating an understanding of genre.

This chapter focuses on several pressing topics related to genre theory, namely concepts of genre, of generic historical patterns, of literary value regarding kinds, of conventions and codes, and of pragmatic uses of genres. Concerning literary discourse, I argue, there is always genre but more than one, which is a methodological permutation of the claim that language is characterized by intertextuality and hetero-glossia. Because genres amalgamate linguistic and social with literary conventions, they are linked with regimes of reason, including the institutional and ideological elements of such cultural formations. Relations between gender and genre bear on this point, revealing among other things the dubious hierarchy of value assigned tradi-tionally to literary kinds from tragedy and epic to gothic fiction and popular romance. As I explain later, I am suspicious of grand sym-metrical historiographies of genre that frame the history of forms in terms of either evolution, devolution, teleology, cyclicality, dialectic continuity, or increasing complexity. Regarding the use of genre in the task of interpretation, I argue for the inescapable polyglot so-ciopolitics of interpretative discourse and against the reductive her-meneutical applications of generic codes as instruments to order and control the meaning of literary texts.

Forms, Conventions, Institutions

Wellek and Warren formulate a set of typical, though problematic, methodological protocols for contemporary genre studies. To start with, "genre should be conceived, we think, as a grouping of literary works based, theoretically, upon both outer form (specific metre or structure) and also upon inner form (attitude, tone, purpose—more crudely, subject and audience)" (231). In addition, "genres can be built up on the basis of inclusiveness or 'richness' as well as that of 'purity' (genre by accretion as well as by reduction)" (235). The effect of genres is to operate as institutional imperatives upon writers and readers: "The literary kind is an 'institution'—as Church, University, or State is an institution" (226). The value of genre studies "is pre-cisely the fact that it calls attention to the internal development of literature"(235).

In their theory of genre, Wellek and Warren create certain prob-lems requiring critical assessment. For instance, the idea that literary kinds should exhibit both structural and thematic distinctive features leads them to dismiss types of literature failing to fit the dual requirement. When push comes to shove, stylistic matters dominate over issues of content—the "conception of genre should lean to the formalistic side, that is, incline to generize Hudibrastic octosyllabics or the sonnet rather than the political novel or the novel about factory workers" (233). Though questionable, their point is that political fiction purportedly lacks a defining stock of devices, whereas poetic kinds like the sonnet foreground just such features. This conclusion, of course, is counterintuitive; academic intellectuals are more likely to recognize as an established genre the political novel than the hudibrastic octosyllabic poem, even without the benefit of having read, say, Howe's *Politics and the Novel.*

One obvious way to avoid Wellek and Warren's problem is, first, to include explicitly as genres identifiable thematic works (for example, epithalamia and strike novels) and, second, to isolate and construe as "devices" distinctive features of plot, tone, character, imagery, and setting. A better solution is to scrap the dysfunctional binary of inner and outer form with its inevitable hierarchizing and prescriptivism. Traits of style, structure, tone, and content can then be merged into the broader category of "convention," which operation effectively insures the mixing of sociohistorical and "literary" dimensions in the definition of genres. (More about the concept of convention will follow in a moment.)

What defines a genre, in part, are identifiable recurring patterns of linguistic, social, stylistic, structural, tonal, presentational, and thematic conventions subject to transformations and linked with certain historical periods and social groups. To put this in broad poststructuralist terms, the heteroglot intertext can be construed as compounded of genres of discourse, and literary genres in this context form an open field amidst the wider cultural archive—the "literary" field intersects with other textual domains like religion, politics, psychology, and the family, which is readily apparent in epics, tragedies, comedies, romances, and so on. This imbrication of literature in regimes of reason is aided by conceiving genres as sets of historical literary conventions joined to linguistic and social conventions. One value of such genre theory, *pace* Wellek and Warren, is to depict the development of literature as consisting of a complex set of often unstable sociohistorical discursive forms in commerce with other discursive forms constituting regimes of reason. In this scheme genre studies attends to the cultural politics of forms as well as to thematic issues, stylistics traits, linguistic features, and sociohistorical discursive matters.

When Wellek and Warren characterize the literary kind as an institution like the church, school, or state, their point is that genres are not biological forms but (wo)manmade historical creations subject to preservation, modification, avoidance, and competition. What actually typifies social institutions like churches, schools, and states are large numbers of "willing" subjects, comparatively vast economic resources, complex hierarchical organizations, known and recognized leaders, sophisticated disciplinary mechanisms, sets of core beliefs and values, complex consensual arrangements, relatively large physical plants, well-trodden paths of cooperation with other such institutions, groupings of satellite sub-institutions, specialized media outlets and spokespersons to disseminate information, heavily invested symbols (flags, color combinations, dress codes), and comparatively ample geographical sites. Few of these characteristics pertain to literary genres. By turning in this manner to the social, Wellek and Warren rely on a superficial and faulty notion of social institutions, simplifying their complex materiality, their networks of power, their mechanisms of authority, and their penchants for normalizing, regularizing, and dominating. Genres are not institutions like churches, schools, or states. To the extent that certain genres display complicated rules for use, or promote specific values, or connect with particular social groups and agencies, however, they are institution-like, but this analogy is both farfetched and misleading. There are, of course, relations between genres and institutions, as, for example, the epic and the state, the drama and the church, the essay and the school, but such linkages are not at all what Wellek and Warren have in mind, being concerned with the aesthetic rather than the ideological aspects of literature. Although genres are not institutions, institutions often employ and frequently regulate particular genres.

Problems of Genealogies and Taxonomies

According to Wellek and Warren's literary historiography, genres may be constructed through accretion or reduction, through "richness" or "purity." An example of the former is the novel, compounded historically of the letter, diary, travel book, character sketch, essay, epic, romance, and comedy. Examples of the latter are not given. They are hard to come by, if they exist at all. One thinks of such kinds as the boasting poem, the character sketch, the curtal sonnet, the short short story, but in each example simpler precursors seem to exist. The idea of genres being composed through a historical process of purification runs counter to the poststructuralist theory of intertextuality, which regards origins as heterogeneous and forms as heteroglot. My critique of Bakhtin's misguided theory of poetry (not the novel), articulated near the close of chapter 3, fleshes out the point. What we encounter here are telling dilemmas related to the genealogy of genre, which for genre studies remains a key area of consideration. On this topic one is reminded of Jolles's protostructuralist notion that complex literary forms derive from simpler elementary kinds like the legend, saga, myth, tale, and joke. One is also mindful of Brunetière's dubious Darwinian model of the evolution of genres subject to processes of natural selection and mutation. Closer to us in time is Shklovsky's suggestive idea that the vitality of "high" genres is constantly renewed through their borrowings from popular literature and mass culture. Theorizing about genre leads characteristically to thoughts about historical patterning—about evolution, devolution, morphology of forms, expansion and purification, return to origins, teleology, cyclicality, and modes of (dis)continuity. With regard to the historicity of genres, I suggest that poststructuralist cultural criticism attend primarily to individual works and constructed sequences of works, but with consideration given to neighboring forms, aberrant and marginal instances, contradictory and subversive traits, minor examples, and inner transformations. To totalize the history of a literary genre or of all genres is to risk recapitulating the authoritarianism of neoclassical theorists with their rigid hierarchies, prescriptivist pronouncements, rules of decorum, and fixations on purity of kind. At the same time, cultural criticism should resist the type of programmatic aestheticism promoted by Croce who regarded each work as unique and who deplored generic classifications. To put this last point in poststructuralist terminology, the loss of the intertext in the name of ultra différance amounts to a foolhardy renunciation: a focus on a particular work should not rule out examining such historical formations as grammatical practices, social codes, author and critic functions, logocentric binaries, and generic conventions. Because genres are sociohistorical discursive constructs partaking in regimes of reason, they are open to productive genealogical inquiry attentive to literary conventions and cultural practices as well as to institutional and ideological matters.

Since there are hundreds of recognized literary kinds, theorists of genre are often drawn to simple taxonomic schemes capable of further secondary elaboration. The classical model, extrapolated out of Aristotle via German Romanticism, is "dramatic, epic, and lyric," where the relationship of the author to the reader supposedly differs in each main type. In our era the dominant model is arguably "fiction, poetry, and drama," each of which is generally regarded as a literary mode rather than a genre per se. Perhaps the most reductive contemporary treatment of this sort occurs among the Chicago critics, with Olson declaring the two major branches of poetics as "mimetic" and "didactic." Literary texts purportedly either present a human activity in a system of probable, necessary, or effective incidents or propound a doctrine or attitude toward a doctrine providing proof of it. The aesthetic outcome is in the former case pleasurable beauty, and in the latter pleasurable instruction. At one point, Olson considers adding a third branch labeled "entertainment" which aims at raw pleasure, but since such literature is frivolous and unreal, he excludes such "swill" from "high art" (588–89). Often the effect of such simplified modeling is to assign to texts and whole regions of discourse specific a priori shaping and unifying principles applicable in the tasks of explication and assessment. In other words, a tendency of theory of modes and genres is to provide reductive protocols for interpretation and evaluation, normalizing and controlling heteroglot literary discourse by specifying beforehand the goal of literary plots, characters, themes, works, and genres.

The hierarchizing phenomenon manifest in Olson is implicit in the general operation of taxonomizing genres. Entertainment is extirpated and so-called minor forms are dismissed. Among critics the epic engenders awe and the diary inspires boredom. From the point of view of contemporary cultural critique, the propensity for literary pedagogy today to focus upon epics that celebrate military prowess and upon aristocratic tragedies that examine the vicissitudes of monarchy is promoted by genre theory still in thrall to classical values. Thus the politics of contemporary genre theory more and more receives and merits suspicion, particularly among such groups as women and African Americans, many of whose literary forms are systematically denigrated. Certain segments of the literary academy exhibit repressive tolerance or contempt for women's diaries, popular romances, slave narratives, and blues. The list of despised genres could be considerably lengthened.

Even as capacious and modulated a system of modes and genres as Frye develops in *Anatomy of Criticism* displays serious limitations and liabilities beyond the occasional fudging of distinctions between certain kinds. As is well known, Frye theorizes a historical pattern of five literary modes in classical and postclassical literature—myth, romance, high mimetic, low mimetic, and irony. Since literature in each mode can be sophisticated or naive and tragic or comic, numerous theoretical combinations are possible: sophisticated comic romance, naive low mimetic tragedy, and so on. Although a work always contains an underlying dominant mode, it can partake of any or all other modes (an instructive observation about generic heterogeneity). Embedded in Frye's idea of the epochal linear progression of modes is the notion that romantic, high mimetic, and low mimetic modes form a series of displaced myths and that irony effects a cyclical movement back toward myth. In this improbable cyclical theory of genre history, myth serves as the *arche* and *telos* of literature. For Frye the bible constitutes the primary source for undisplaced myth in the postclassical Western tradition. It holds a singularly privileged place, being a major source of our images, symbols, character types, plots, tropes, and genres. The outcome of this theorizing is to provide a complex systematics for genre theory and to tie this system to religious myth as ground and source. To make myth and religion the foundation of literature, Frye employs a highly questionable recursive historiography of genre. Despite all his ingenuity, he ends up largely confirming the reigning definitions and axiologies of traditional genres.

While Frye helpfully frames literature as a collective communal phenomenon possessing inherent connections with utopian thinking, he frequently sacrifices history in the process. For instance, historical conventions often give way massively to archetypes. Consider the following complex example. To empower his concept of the bible as source myth, Frye has to dismiss the higher criticism of the bible, which examines stages of composition, textual redactions, scribal insertions, editorial conflations, and corruptions in transmission. He advocates instead a "synthetizing process which would start with the assumption that the Bible is a definitive myth, a single archetypal structure extending from creation to apocalypse. Its heuristic principle would be St. Augustine's axiom that the Old Testament is revealed in the New and the New concealed in the Old. . . . We cannot trace the Bible back, even historically, to a time when its materials were not being shaped into a typological unity" (315). For Frye the bible is a single unified coherent myth organized around the heroic quest of the central figure, Messiah. It is not a mishmash of texts joined together through millennium-long processes of editing. This outcome depends on setting aside textual and historical criticism and employing strategies developed by patristic typological hermeneutics in order to confer upon both biblical testaments pristine originality and priority. Thus, the bible becomes for Western culture the central well of archetypes. The ethnocentric omission of all Western traditions but certain patriarchal Christian ones, the obvious violence done to Jewish traditions, and the dangerous preferences for synthesis and unity at all costs make this ambitious archetypal "genre theory" highly suspect.

Although he is indebted to Frye, Todorov sets out to improve on his precursor. Sounding very much the scientific structuralist, Todorov proclaims, "We should posit, on the one hand, *historical genres;* on the other, *theoretical genres.* The first would result from an observation of literary reality; the second from a deduction of a theoretical order" (13–14). For Todorov the main problem with Frye is not that his system is composed of theoretical genres (quite the contrary), but that he is inconsistent and lacking in logical rigor. As Todorov notes, "Many possible combinations are missing from Frye's enumeration" (13). For genre studies Todorov promotes a theoretical rather than a historical approach. In his view, "historical genres form a part of the complex theoretical genres" (15). To construct genres one needs some abstract properties and some laws governing relations of properties. Given meter, rhyme, and theme, for example, one can construct innumerable genres. The sonnet is a possibility. So too is, let us say, a ten-line poem alternating two and three anapestic feet rhyming *a b c d e,* celebrating the woes in marriage. Let us call it an anti-epithalamium and project a sequence of them. Perhaps we may uncover precursor poems leading up to this new literary kind. What is suggestive and liberating in Todorov, as in Frye, is the theoretical manner of thinking about genre. Innumerable combinations can be fruitfully projected. Knowing there is detective fiction in the nineteenth century and a lively feminist movement, one can posit that there are probably feminist (sub)versions of the genre. It turns out that, indeed, there are. Perhaps there exist African-American (sub)versions. I don't know. New genres, of course, emerge all the time. One thinks of rap, blues, concrete poetry, *Dinggedichte.* One can project the computer poem or the interactive illustrated video poem in color. Perhaps they already exist. One is mindful of Empson framing as versions of pastoral *As You Like It, The Beggar's Opera,* and *Alice in Wonderland,* an inventive generic grouping. Todorov's resolute advocacy of theoretical genres engenders a creative sense of play regarding genre, which is helpful in counteracting the confining neoclassical solemnity still surrounding historicist thinking about genre.

Like Wellek and Warren, Todorov becomes involved with historiography when distinguishing the concept of genre (or species) as employed in biology from that used in methodological studies like science and literary criticism. If one knows the species called tiger, notes Todorov, one can infer from it the characteristics of each tiger. The arrival of a new tiger does not change the definition of the species.

> The same is not the case in the realm of art or of science. Here evolution operates with an altogether different rhythm: *every* work modifies the sum of possible works, each new example alters the species. . . . More exactly, we grant a text the right to figure in the history of literature or of science only insofar as it produces a change in our previous notion of the one activity or the other. Texts that do not fulfill this condition automatically pass into another category: that of so-called popular or mass literature in the one case; in the other, that of the academic exercise or unoriginal experiment. . . . Only "popular" literature (detective stories, serialized novels, science fiction, etc.) would approach fulfilling the requirements of genre in the sense the word has in natural science; for the notion of genre in that sense would be inapplicable to strictly literary texts. (6)

This traditionalist view of literary genre is fully in league with "great works" concepts of literature. Only works capable of redirecting, redefining, or somehow significantly changing their genres are worthy of a place in literary history. Other works are dross, consigned to the inferior category of the "popular" or the "mass." The process of sorting the truly "literary" from the "popular" is done, according to Todorov, "automatically." This claim is, of course, outrageous. So too is the claim that each literary work modifies its genre. Does *every* sonnet transform the genre sonnet? Because he is committed to a retrograde aesthetic theory that defines each "work" as, in part, unique, Todorov must consign much of the history of literature to the scrap heap of the "mass." He would have us believe that most detective stories, serialized novels, and science fiction conform fully to generic rules and that, therefore, they are aesthetically unworthy. What Todorov truly values from an aesthetic historiographical point of view is "descriptive" study of successful mutations—"strong works." Such an exclusionary program for genre studies is of little use to cultural criticism, which regards the scrutiny of mass and popular genres at least as important as the study of so-called masterworks.

Amalgamations and Anomalies

Employing yet extending the structuralist concepts of "codes" and "conventions," I want to move beyond Todorov in the conceptualization of genre. An observation by Scholes in *Textual Power* offers a helpful beginning. He points out that "a text is to its genre as the speech act is to its language. The genre is a network of codes that can be inferred from a set of related texts. . . . No one who has ever studied seriously the history of any art can doubt the importance of precedent, schema, presupposition, convention . . . " (2). Using the concepts of code and convention, I wish to expand the framework for understanding genre. The rules of genre generally deal with literary codes and conventions concerning characterization, plot, setting, imagery, tone, structure, prosody, style, theme, point of view, etc. And it goes without saying that linguistic conventions and codes having to do with syntax, phonology, semantics, and tropology also play formative roles in the construction of literary genres. Finally, social codes and conventions are indispensable in generic formations: the writing and reading of novels, plays, poems, and other literary texts are entangled with conventions and codes related to such matters as dress, hygiene, courtesy, cuisine, punctuality, conversation, social interactions, vocational duties, leisure activities, financial obligations, family relations, religious worship, legal liability, citizenship responsibility, ethical judgment, and aesthetic appreciation. The point is the construction of genres involves the amalgamation of literary, linguistic, and social codes and conventions. Where Scholes portrays a text as a speech act and its genre as a language, I take a step back to depict genres as concatenations of literary, linguistic, and social codes and conventions and their matrices as regimes of reason. For me, the primary enabling condition of genre is the archive of culture. An adequate definition of any genre, therefore, would take into account a plurality of codes and conventions, just as it would address phenomena of blurring, continuity, and transformation.

Poststructuralists and structuralists alike regard the terms *code, convention,* and *practice* as rough synonyms. I concur. In each case the mechanism at work links a particular habitual or regular occurrence with a broader system. Examples include speech → language, text → genre, genre → cultural archive. From this vantage, one important task of cultural criticism is to connect literary discourses and genres with regimes of reason, which include networks of institutions that facilitate and constitute regimes. It is, therefore, not enough to frame genre studies as a move from genre to literary system; the literary system itself must tie in with cultural systems.

In working with codes, conventions, practices, and their processes of transformation, cultural criticism engages in textual exegesis, institutional analysis, and ideological critique. On this last point structuralism and poststructuralism are at odds, for structuralism aspires to scientific neutrality, which in the domain of genre studies presents itself as a desire to engage in pure description of deep structures. In analyzing the constitution of systems, poststructuralism generally investigates such matters as the installation of defining binary oppositions, the arbitrariness and undecidability of boundaries, the deployments of power and authority, the points of transformation and breakage, the (de)construction of stabilities and metalanguages, and the fissures wrought by the unconscious. In the area of genre studies this leads to interest in anomalous generic mechanisms and functions with an eye toward rules of formation and exclusion, impositions of hierarchies, fabrications of marginal forms, flights of meaning, contradictions and paradoxes, slippages of control, returns of repressed materials, and evidences of heterogeneity. Paradigmatic events in the poststructuralist analysis of generic discourse include the eruption of the heteroglot intertext, the apparition of omissions, the collapse of traditional frames, and the rhetorical subversion of tropological codes. What poststructuralism does, then, is to question the assured status and authority ascribed to discursive genres, not their existence nor their necessity.

"Pragmatics" of Genre

In arguing for a revised theory of genre, Rosmarin claims that "a genre is chosen or defined to fit neither a historical nor a theoretical reality but to serve a pragmatic end" (49–50). Here genre serves as a critical instrument invented solely for interpretation. To the extent that a reading is rich and persuasive, its use of genre is justified and valuable. The proper direction of genre theory is from purposeful description of genre to exegetical revelation of text: "It is not an attempt to imitate a 'horizontal' historical reality, an 'intrinsic' textual reality, a 'theoretical' genre, or the process by which the critic actually 'discovered' his argument" (42). Self-consciously, this neopragmatist view discounts hermeneutical, formalist, and structuralist accounts of genre. In its desire to gain interpretative power over individual texts, it knowingly sacrifices critical scope, narrowly constructing the scenario of criticism and explicitly putting the author, milieu, and text in positions of subordination to the will and strategy of the ambitious critic-exegete who defines in order to explicate/exploit generic discourse. In all this nothing much is disturbed in the institution of academic literary criticism—the strong reading of the canonical text in competition with other readings survives intact. Critical language mixes with and orients literary language in a process not of identification but of domination. Critique appears out of the question since the critic is, by definition, complicitous with texts.

It is revealing that Rosmarin writes in the 1980s yet finds nothing significant for genre theory in the concept of convention. In *Structuralist Poetics,* for example, Culler observes about conventions of interpretation: "One can think of these conventions not simply as the implicit knowledge of the reader but also as the implicit knowledge of authors. To write a poem or a novel is immediately to engage with a literary tradition or at the very least with a certain idea of the poem or the novel. The activity is made possible by the existence of the genre, which the author can write against, certainly, whose conventions he may attempt to subvert, but which is none the less the context within which his activity takes place"(116). Genres' conventions, often unconscious or implicit, shape the labors of authors and critics alike—

even if such constituents of tradition are under attack. Here the notion of convention keeps in play for critical inquiry concepts of the author, the critic, the text, the tradition(s), the transformation of codes, and the unconscious. However it is construed, the idea of convention operates as a magnetic nodal point, attracting to itself numerous filaments of discursive systems and of critical theorizing. A pragmatic theory of genre with no care for conventions seems needlessly impoverished, as indeed Rosmarin's appears on this score.

Parenthetically, it is characteristic of some contemporary genre theory to focus on canonical works and kinds and to display indifference or contempt for noncanonical texts and forms. This occurs in a world where new as well as traditional aesthetic practices increasingly permeate everyday life, collapsing the boundaries between high and low art, fixed and hybrid kinds, and literary and nonliterary forms. Some critics among us regard this whole tendency—which is certainly not peculiar to our era—as lamentable, profane mongrelization. Exuberant eruptions of heteroglossia and intertextuality appear anathema to guardians of the pure and noble who dot the ranks of genre theorists in noticeable numbers. It is evident that the shaping power of the imagination manifests itself in large-scale shopping malls as much as in grand epics and that prized literary devices and traditions are regularly mined by writers and directors of television shows, movies, and advertising spots. Ordinary existence is everywhere and commonly striated with aesthetic elements of literary discourse. The autonomy of literature seems a ridiculous dream. In these circumstances, it is possible to think that the extension of literary analysis to the cultural text, broadly construed, appears almost inevitable and even promising, provided it is not limited to technical analysis. The developments in narratology, which is not focused on fiction but on all narratives (literature, history, cinema, television, painting), make this area of genre inquiry something of a vanguard. The work of White, examined in chapter 3, remains exemplary in the wide-ranging linkages of historical narratives with literary genres, rhetorical figures, logical forms, and ideological orientations. Among contemporary literary intellectuals continued scorn for noncanonical, nontraditional, and "unliterary" forms, both recently reclaimed and emergent ones, has to be construed as narrowly conservative and elitist, likely to be hostile to any enterprise of cultural criticism, if not indifferent through inertia.

Theory of genre is typically treated as a branch of poetics, which is how Wellek and Warren, Frye, and Todorov handle it. Because Rosmarin regards genre theory from the vantage of critical practice, she shifts the matter of literary kinds to the issue of critical types— each of which construes genres as befits its programs. This shift does not simplify the problematics of genre, rather it resituates them in the vexed domain of interpretive theory. Unfortunately, Rosmarin refuses inquiry into modes of criticism, being preoccupied with mounting new interpretations of certain canonical dramatic monologues and mask lyrics. To counter this turn I had recourse, with Culler's help, to the concept of convention where literary conventions were presented as *both* poetic *and* critical protocols. In order to examine further the consequences of a pragmatics rather than a poetics of genre, I want to scrutinize Lyotard's work in this area.

Lyotard fixes his attention upon the effects of interpretative "genres" in the social constructions and political applications of discourse, paying no particular heed to "literary" kinds. His main concern is with the genres of discourse in general and with the *différends* (disputes) among such genres. Focused methodologically on the "phrase" and its modes of linkage, his theory usefully depicts the occurrence of one or more phrases as the emergence of a social universe consisting of addressor, addressee, referent, and meaning. "It could be said that the social is given immediately with a phrase universe . . . and that it is given as immediately determined by, in principle, the regimen of that phrase, even though its determination is straightway the object of another phrase, whose linking on cannot help but be the occasion for differends between genres of discourse. It could be said for that very reason that politics is immediately given with a phrase as a differend to be regulated concerning the matter of the means of linking onto it. It is just as pointless to ask questions about the 'origin' of the political as it is about the social. The social is impli-

cated in the universe of a phrase and the political in its mode of linking" (140–41). For Lyotard the making of phrases summons the social, and the operation of connecting one phrase with another (or
others) in the likelihood of dispute originates politics. In situating
this sociopolitics of discourse, Lyotard singles out for attention two
distinct sites where contentions occur—on the level of the phrase and
on the level of the genres of discourse. Putting together sequences of
phrases involves linking heterogeneous "phrase regimens" like knowing, describing, questioning, recounting, ordering, prescribing, and
describing. In the operation of linking there are gaps covered over not
only among phrase regimens but also among genres of discourse such
as the economic, scientific, ethical, philosophical, dialectic, erotic,
declarative, speculative, narrative, and escatological. By definition a
genre of discourse links incompatible phrases and phrase regimens in
the interests of certain values and goals. Among genres of discourse
disputes unavoidably flare as different strategies and stakes contend
with one another. Despite the incommensurabilities begetting numerous differends, genres of discourse can become hegemonic, as did
the dialectical genre in classical Greece, the technical genre during
the Industrial Revolution, and the economic genre for advanced
capitalism. "The stakes bound up with a genre of discourse determine
the linkings between phrases. They determine them, however, only as
an end may determine the means: by eliminating those that are not
opportune" (84).

What can Lyotard's portrait of phrases and discursive genres as a
polyglot and polygeneric struggle add to contemporary theory of
genre and to cultural criticism? Since Lyotard does not address such
matters, one must extrapolate consequences. With Lyotard the concept of genre migrates from the (literary) text, atomized into a
hodgepodge of heterogeneous phrases and regimens, to critical discourse. Kinds of criticism coopt the concept of genre, and the genres
of critical discourse are characterized by their different interests,
goals, and programs. The social universe of the text necessarily undergoes political constructions. When a text is assigned a genre, the as-
signment is typically at the hands of criticism and it is enacted as an

interested political intervention. Genres of criticism can become hegemonic, as did New Criticism in the postwar period. Significantly, a writer/scriptor does "generize" heterogeneous phrases and regimens in a critical sociopolitical operation effecting exclusions, omissions, and suppressions. Here the critical process infiltrates the so-called labor of creativity, conditioning the production of texts in a political manner. Pragmatics loops back into poetics. The author of a text is just another critic—with similar rights of use. A text is always more than a genre allows, and this surplus is incorrigible for no genre can totally saturate all the phrases and gaps in a text.

For critics and writers alike genre emerges, in Lyotard's treatment, as an inescapable and seemingly sinister convenience: generic ends justify exclusionary means. Where Todorov's heuristic model of theoretical genres dissipates the solemnity surrounding the history of genres, Lyotard's theory of genre undermines any confidence conventions of genre might afford. Literary discourse cannot escape genres; it experiences genres as insistent (pre)conditions inadequate to its complex textuality. In all of this, conventions emerge not as neutral devices but as political instruments insuring order, effecting exclusions, and carrying out programs.

Questions of Gender

Significant work has been done on the relations of gender and genre, raising questions for contemporary genre studies. One is mindful of recent feminist studies of gothic fictions, women's utopias, female science fictions, and popular romantic fictions, all of which genres employ fantasy to subvert the patriarchal symbolic orders of modern societies. In the case of popular romance, to limit the illustrations, debate continues over the ideology of the genre as to whether primarily it transgresses puritanical rules restraining women's desire, or confirms prevailing standards pertaining to monogamous heterosexual marriage, or provides pleasurable release from the dissatisfactions of domestic heterosexual norms, or reduces the world to a few people in a private sphere of spiritualized sexuality. Work has been carried out on the formula of this fiction, the publishing industry's role in shaping the market, and the broad readership in America and abroad. Batsleer and others associated with the Birmingham Centre for Contemporary Cultural Studies have examined "masculine romances" (westerns, war stories, thrillers, spy novels, detective stories, boys' adventures), isolating for attention recurring patterns of male solidarity and camaraderie, masculine sexual identity, and mastery of public space. Such work as is mentioned here exemplifies how genres can usefully be studied as cultural forms/formulas lodged at the intersection of "literature," ideology, institutions, and gender roles. We are a long way from Wellek and Warren's strictures about defining genres mainly in terms of stylistic traits.

In relation to *écriture féminine* and to the (maternal) genotext, discussed in chapter 3, provocative questions arise as to whether such special gender-inflected writings are generic, nongeneric, antigeneric, polygeneric, or pregeneric. Can one imagine discourse as nongeneric or pregeneric? Doesn't poststructuralism predispose one to frame all writing as polygeneric, i.e., heteroglot and intertextual? Don't Cixous, Kristeva, and other French feminists conceive "feminine" writings like *écriture féminine* and the genotext explicitly against preexisting patriarchal categories, including genre classifications? Associated with rules and the social symbolic, aren't genres by definition under the name of the father?

Just as the phrase for Lyotard and the trope for White appear to be pregeneric linguistic entities, the same seems to be the case with Cixous' *écriture féminine* and Kristeva's genotext. Neither Lyotard nor White, however, presents phrases and tropes as autonomous monads; they are ultimately bound to (variable) genres as conditions of emergence in discourse. Language variously institutes the social, political, cognitive, and generic. What Cixous and Kristeva advocate is avantgarde writing that is not pregeneric but antigeneric, meaning antipatriarchal. This writing is construed as nongeneric to the extent that it doesn't yet exist, except in fleeting and irregular prophetic patches of texts. Because the theory of feminine writing promotes libidinal overflows, it fosters polygeneric discourse. As it summons gynocentric universes, such writing engenders sociopolitical tropes and phrases, which are discursive practices on their way to becoming anticonventional or nonconventional conventions. Revolutionary work, in literature as in politics, is in large measure coded activity. Often enough the creative element consists in new arrangements and combinations of old materials.

My conclusions are that gender studies pose powerful challenges to traditional genre studies, that gender-marked writing cannot elude the problematics of genre conventions and genres, that revolutions in "literary" language partake of regimes of reason, that the gendering of genres effectively subverts key values and hierarchies of existing generic canons, and that gender-based genre studies facilitates inroads into a broad critique of institutionalized literary studies.

Transformations of Genre Studies

In bringing this chapter to a close, I want to offer a proposition—with literary discourse there is always genre but more than one. The amalgamation of linguistic, aesthetic, and social codes that characterizes the formation of a literary kind insures both heteroglot and polygeneric texts, even if they are parsimoniously so. Put differently, the invasion of the text by the intertext and the social text undercuts considerations of non- or pregeneric uniqueness or of generic purity, which are faulty aestheticist ideals. The idea of poetic rarefaction depends on the quotidian archive; examples of such aesthetic paragons can be shown to be grounded in everyday discourse. The sacred and profane are not simply neighbors but kissing cousins, moving within and among conventions of regimes of reason. Neither operates beyond institutions and ideologies. Furthermore, phrases get caught up in multiple sociopolitical struggles.

Poststructuralist cultural criticism need deny neither the existence nor pertinence of literary genres. It does, however, question the aesthetic hierarchies and the symmetrical historiographies of traditional genre theories. My argument can be regarded as another manifestation of the contemporary critique of the Enlightenment legacy, particularly its classicist axiology. The retrieval of despised, forgotten, minor, and marginal genres, the attack on the canon, the attraction to heteroglossia and pastiche, the preoccupation with permeable generic boundaries, and the revaluation of popular and mass forms all testify not to the end of genre but to significant transformations of genre studies. Today national epics and aristocratic verse tragedies seem remote (if "foundational") curiosities very much in service to a sexist, racist, and classist status quo. Cast as rule-bound forms, prescriptive literary genres impose controls on (inter)textuality. To circumvent this factitious tendency of genre theory, poststructuralism deploys pluralized conventions in characterizing generic discourses. The emphasis here falls upon discontinuity and hodgepodge, not continuity and purity. This explains why, in arguing against Wellek and Warren, I recommend during the initial process of defining the stocks of devices for genres that critics take into account without discrimination conventions of theme, tone, character, setting, purpose, and audience as well as of meter, rhyme, plot, imagery, point of view, design, and figurative language. By initially scrapping the form/content binary, one avoids the predisposition to privilege certain properties and combinations of properties over others, and one resists the lure of purification rituals in the task of depicting genres, whether they be historical or theoretical or pragmatic. Given the complex historical sedimentations constituting conventions, genres can generally be shown to be unstable heterogeneous formations capable of following out multiple lines of development. There is a need not to jettison genre studies but to transform its guiding concepts of genre, historiography, value, convention, and interpretation.

However modulated a poetics of genre may be, the hermeneutic applications of generic formulations tend toward simplifications and reductions. Given the tendency of some genre critics to favor single pure forms and coherent aesthetic outcomes, the work of critical interpretation characteristically runs several risks, including severing the connections of generic texts to supporting institutions, overlooking surrounding sociopolitical struggles in the conflicts of interpretation, and suppressing the polygeneric features of literary discourse. Genres can broaden critical understanding, though they often don't do so, serving instead as reductive protocols leading the efforts at exegesis and evaluation to predictable ends. Used as efficient tools for interpretations, genre schemas rein in or exclude centrifugal elements. Such legislative dictums as uttered by Hirsch, for example, represent this common disorder of genre pragmatics: "valid interpretation is always governed by a valid inference about genre" (113) and "the concept of genre cuts through all particular varieties of biblical, poetical, historical, and legal interpretation of texts because the notion of genre in itself determines an intrinsic mode of proceeding" (263). Each text has a defining genre; get it right and valid textual interpretation is assured. To get the genre right is to avoid the "lawlessness of textual commentary from the heyday of Alexandria to the present" (127). Here genre insures control of texts through a controlling generic interpretation, and hermeneutics overcomes heteroglossia. Programmatically, there is always genre but only one. On the contrary, however, the play of multiple generic devices in the heteroglot (inter)text undermines the credibility of the severe legal strictures and critical controls desired by conservative hermeneuticists; so too do other textual complications wrought by contending social conventions and aberrant linguistic codings, particularly incompatible phrase regimens, grammatical gaps, and figural oscillations. It is a delusion to believe that genre settles hermeneutical disputes; the opposite is more nearly the case.

5

Pluralizing Poetics

Contemporary theories of literature relating to ethnic enclaves, oppressed groups, and colonized peoples call into question traditional claims for a single universal poetics applicable to all humanity. From this perspective the capacious poetics outlined by Frye appears as a Christianized Eurocentric model that bears little, if any, direct relevance to numerous literatures. There is not one but a plurality of poetics. The pluralizing of poetics characteristic of recent decades is often linked with political forces advocating decentralization and self-determination as well as with social forces promoting subgroup unity and purification. Not surprisingly, theories of minority literatures exhibit complicated clusters of mixed motives and goals, particularly regarding the ethicopolitical dimensions of aesthetic doctrines. To construct an account of poetics suited to poststructuralist cultural criticism, I find it helpful in this chapter to explore minoritarian literary theories developed by black aestheticians, feminists, and anticolonial thinkers. Also in this discussion I scrutinize the suggestive reflections on "minor literature" offered by Deleuze and Guattari and the observations on "marginality" made by de Certeau. I focus on theories of minority literatures not because this area of research in poetics is still too little regarded by academic literary intellectuals, but because my own understanding of poetics derives, in large part, from minority theories.

In the poetics being developed throughout this book, I have argued that literary discourse is at once rhetorical, heteroglot, and intertextual, conditioned by institutions and interests that partake in and of regimes of reason. Texts are authored by subjects, divided and in process, whose bodies/beings are situated at particular sites of regimes and who speak for certain unconscious and conscious interests. Moreover, texts are heterogeneous discursive constructs, by turns inventive and banal, that amalgamate linguistic and archival codes and conventions and that produce continuities and discontinuities, rendering referentiality uncertain. The constituents of "literature" in one place and time need not duplicate such elements in other locales and moments. Because the labor of defining (a) "literature" entails inclusions and exclusions in line with certain values and interests, the domain of poetics is an arena of contestation. There is no ontology of literature per se; there are literature functions in relation to particular regimes and programs. Racist, patriarchal, and colonial regimes characteristically denigrate, exclude, or overlook "minority literatures" produced by people of color, women, and "natives," all of whom must struggle against the effects of domination. The poetics of minorities emerge from heterogeneous, conflictual regimes, divided, oppressed subjects, and hybrid language traditions and cultural intertexts, which we shall consider in this chapter.

Black Aesthetics in America

To start let me rehearse briefly some of the historical background to the arguments launched by American black aestheticians. During the revolutionary period when the Declaration of Independence and the Constitution of the United States were written, the quarter of the population that was black was not included. From the outset several centuries ago, the fate of black people in North America involved deportation, slavery, oppression, and struggle. In the pre–Civil War era black leaders like Douglass advocated social reform and racial integration while others like Delany recommended black nationalism. At the turn of the century Garvey promoted the return of black Americans to Africa, whereas Washington argued that black citizenship in America should be attained gradually by hard work, vocational education, and moral improvement. Later Du Bois demanded redress from white

America and sought immediate political enfranchisement. These contending political programs—conciliation and integration, reform and redress, nationalism and freedom in Africa—rooted in early American history, reemerged in the black liberation movement spanning the years from the close of the Korean War to the end of the Vietnam War. What typifies the early years of the civil rights struggle are resistance to segregation, the upsurge of nonviolent protest organizations, the goal of racial integration, and the attainment of limited successes in the courts and news media. The later years, the days of the black power movement, are characterized by riots and armed resistance rather than passive nonviolence, by preoccupation with addressing economic impoverishment more than legal rights, by dedication to political autonomy and black statehood instead of integration, and by celebrations of racial pride, negritude, and Africanism in place of submission to institutionalized Euro-American conventions, norms, and standards. It is the poetics emerging from this latter phase of cultural struggle that I wish to consider here.

Gayle, Henderson, Baker, and others argue that black people in America have a whole distinctive and separate way of life that is neither Anglo-Saxon nor African. African-American folk elements and artistic forms, manifestations of a historically molded black unconscious or "soul," exhibit, for instance, a collectivistic rather than an individualistic ethos, a repudiative rather than an accommodative psychology, and an oral-musical rather than a textual tradition of discourse. As suggested by its folktales, songs, sermons, blues, and jazz, the black community in America constitutes an internal colony, possessing its own cultural values, styles, voices, customs, themes, techniques, and genres.

Not unexpectedly, the use of mainstream cultural values and criteria to assess minority forms of life typically "finds" such vernacular forms to be grotesque, humorous, paranoid, "entertaining," inferior. The application of white Eurocentric standards often leads to the denigration of African-American modes of being and expression. Just as the whole culture of black America is distinct and different from white America, so the black arts in their authentic forms are, and should continue to be, separate. Simply put, this is the general thrust of the black aesthetic in a moderate form. There are more radical versions, as the work of Baraka illustrates.

Writing to American blacks, Baraka declares, "We are a people. We are unconscious captives unless we realize this—that we have always been separate, except in our tranced desire to be the thing that oppressed us"(240). The task of elevating black consciousness entails exorcising the hegemonic white regime of reason, which must be replaced by a black regime fashioned, in part, by artists.

> The Black artist, in this context, is desperately needed to change the images his people identify with, by asserting Black feeling, Black mind, Black judgment. The Black intellectual, in the same context, is needed to change the interpretations of facts toward the Black Man's best interests, instead of merely tagging along reciting white judgments of the world.
>
> Art, Religion, and Politics are impressive vectors of a culture. Art describes a culture. Black artists must have an image of what the Black sensibility is in this land. Religion elevates a culture. The Black Man must aspire to Blackness. God is man idealized. The Black Man must idealize himself as Black. And idealize and aspire to that. Politics give a social order to the culture, i.e., make relationships within the culture definable for the functioning organism. The Black Man must seek a Black politics, an ordering of the world that is beneficial to his culture, to his interiorization and judgment of the world. (248)

In Baraka's scheme, the African-American artist is part of a cultural avant-garde whose mission is to bring about social transformation in the interest of black empowerment and liberation. The program involves pragmatically altering politics and religion as well as the arts. A fourfold poetics for black liberation emerges: art accurately depicts life; art instructs the audience; art elevates social consciousness; art derives from the community for the community. This stipulative ethicopolitical poetics, formulated in very traditional terms, is, however, radically premised on the imposed separate and inferior status of black Americans. In Baraka's words, "Black People are a race, a culture, a

Nation" (248). Race comes first. Upon that essential base the artist helps construct authentic national culture.

It is not surprising that contemporary black aestheticians find much in the history of canonical African-American literature to criticize. In the past numerous black writers were captivated by the dominant criteria and values of the white world. Speaking of the Harlem Renaissance, for instance, Neal complains, "It did not address itself to the mythology and the life-styles of the Black community. It failed to take roots, to link itself concretely to the struggles of that community, to become its voice and spirit" (39). Perhaps the most dire consequence of this line of thinking would be to extirpate "racial traitors" from the canon. Something like this is foreshadowed in the battles among black critics over the work of Ellison. When Baraka argues dramatically that the "changing of images, of references, is the Black Man's way back to the racial integrity of the captured African, which is where we must take ourselves" (247), he makes racial purity a paramount political and aesthetic touchstone. In this connection, declares Baraka, the black bourgeoisie in America were long ago "created in the image of white people, as they still are, and wanted nothing to do with Black" (242). At its most radical, the poetics of the black aesthetic theorists rests on a revolutionary racial ethicopolitics, which finds it necessary to take sanctions against certain black individuals and groups in the name of the emergent black people and nation.

To counter the violent wish among black aestheticians for purification, I would argue that the black "nation" in America, systematically deported, enslaved, and colonized, consists of a heterogeneous mass of peoples stemming from different African tribes, language groups, religions, economic backgrounds, and body types. To take recourse in concepts of original pre-diaspora pan-African unity, therefore, is to engage in fantasy and fiction, creating a mythical essentialism of "pure Africanism" improbably shared by all people of African descent and magically capable now of uniting them. In my view, the purging of several centuries of history, an impossible mass cleansing, will not lead back to pure African ethnicity—one capable of establishing an autonomous, unified nation. While I am opposed to neither a separatist politics nor a separatist poetics based on sociohistorical as well as "racial" factors, I find the essentialist appeal to racial integrity and pan-African cultural unity insubstantial and dangerous. It is a case of regressive allegorizing where what is needed is progressive novelizing.

The thinking about poetics among some radical black aestheticians relies upon certain dubious polemical formulations, particularly regarding the idea of "nation" (not to mention the questionable concept of "race"). Despite many utopian prognostications that nationalism would eventually die out, new nations have proliferated in our time. While the concept of nation today appears inescapable, its progressive use seems to have no guarantees. In Baraka's account, for example, there exists in America a black race of people with its own culture, which forms the foundation for the maturing of a black "nation" complete with sovereign and autonomous land, military force, judicial system, and diplomatic corps. As Baraka presents it, there is at once a black nation in existence and a black nation to come: "We do not want a Nation, we are a Nation" (239); and "it is impossible to be a Nationalist without talking about land" (242). His poetics is tied to the enterprise of nation-building: the three tasks of the poet are to solidify what exists (a "people") through consciousness-raising, encourage wresting a sovereign domain from white people, and lead the people in this struggle. To create the new nation, "the first act must be the nationalization of all properties and resources belonging to white people, within the boundaries of the Black Nation" (249). Membership in the black nation, as both state of mind and autonomous place of dwelling, is evidently not accorded to whites, to integrationists (black or white), or to members of the black middle class who avoid blacks and identify with whites. Ideally, the new nation will have citizens who are physically, psychologically, and politically "black." "By the time this book appears," boasts Baraka in his collection of social essays, "I will be even blacker"(10). "Black" constitutes the metaphysical essence of the black nation as well as the black aesthetic; it is ultimately a hypostatized metaphorical entity at once capable of quantification yet immaterial. But "black," as constituted by Baraka, provides an inadequate and fantastical foundation for a theory of "nationhood" and an account of culture.

In fact, Baraka elides "nation" and "state." As I see it, the creation of a sovereign land and political entity calls for the establishment of a (new) "state." The basis for this state is the existence of a nation or, better yet, a "people"—a material mode of collective life and communal frame of mind (conscious and unconscious), all formed by the historical inscription of slavery and its aftermath. Significantly, long-standing elements of the (national) experience of the people include the integrationist and meliorist projects, which, however, the new state rules out. The point is that the "state" emerges out of the violent and exclusionary purification of the "nation." Baraka obfuscates such distinctions.

There are, of course, many black literatures and there are many black nations and states. To summon some of the complexities in this area, I want to expand briefly on Gates's helpful intertextual theory of text-milieu. Building on Gates, I shall sketch an account of minority poetics from the perspective of poststructuralist cultural theory. Gates observes that a black literature written in a Western language, whether English, French, Portuguese, or Spanish, is heir to 1) a standard language, tradition, and canon derived from Greco-Roman, Judeo-Christian, and European cultures and 2) a vernacular language, tradition, and emerging canon descended from African, Caribbean, or African-American cultures. The white heritage of written discourse is part of an oppressive, ethnocentric colonial order, unlike the black legacy of native oral discourse. For Gates the job of minority criticism is to draw upon and diverge from mainstream traditions and to delve into and derive principles and practices from marginal traditions. Surprisingly, he deemphasizes the Muslim half of the African populace, which renders many traditions of African art potentially triple-stranded. The poetics intimated by Gates and advocated here casts a black literature as a heterogeneous intertextual compound rather than a homogeneous oral instantiation of racial essence. Such a poetics does not attempt to decolonize literature or culture either by purging elements of standard traditions or by getting back to pre-exilic African tribal orality. Black literatures are, by definition, heteroglot discourses created by colonized minority cultures composed of separated and separate, oppressed peoples. This poetics conceptualizes rather than expunges the many-strandedness of black literatures. What defines black literatures, to employ Bhabha's term, is "hybridity" (7).

Obviously, I am not advocating a renewal of Tainean cultural criticism. To be specific, I do not believe that the foundation and central source of art is racial or national disposition. I do not encourage critics to write psychohistories of "organic civilizations." And I do not promote the notion that readers either can or should pass rapidly beyond discourse to direct communion with racial essence. Although important in relating literature to society, Taine's is a flawed endeavor, offering little of use to poststructuralist cultural criticism.

Women's Literatures

It is revealing that Baraka and others during the heyday of the black power movement continually refer to the "Black Man," omitting mention of black women. As black feminists point out, black male critics, radicals and moderates, nationalists and integrationists, regularly "forget" black women. The formation of numerous black feminist groups in the United States, especially the National Black Feminist Organization, bears witness to an emergent autonomous movement among African-American women, who must struggle with both black men and white men and women. In the latter case, white feminist organizations do not represent the interests of black women. Many black women find closer allies with women of color and Third World women than with white women because for them the issue of gender is inextricably enmeshed with the issues of class and race. Within the racial ghettos of contemporary colonial and neocolonial societies, the economic, familial, and political situations of many Third World women of color have much in common. White women inhabit another world. Not surprisingly, when Barbara Smith outlines a project for black feminist literary study, she explicitly links gender, race, and class: "A Black feminist approach to literature that embodies the realization that the politics of sex as well as the politics of race and class are crucially interlocking factors in the works of Black women writers is an absolute necessity" (170).

Among contemporary African-American literary women it is common to regard black women's literature as having its own special poetics and its own traditions. As Smith phrases it, "Thematically, stylistically, aesthetically, and conceptually Black women writers manifest common approaches to the act of creating literature" (174) and "Black women writers constitute an identifiable literary tradition" (174). This special minority poetics is constructed against the backdrop of struggles with black men and white women, that is, black feminist poetics self-consciously differs from the black aesthetic (which is a male formulation) and from the white female aesthetic (which is a racist and classist construction). Among American minority literatures, in other words, is the literature of black women— which should not be subsumed by the neighboring categories of either black (male) literature or (white) women's literature.

It is perhaps arguable whether the literatures of white women in Western societies also constitute "minority literatures" given the numerical superiority of white women in such societies. However, the fact that exceedingly few such women writers enter into the canons of great works suggests a fairly uniform social status tantamount to minority status. To put this another and more direct way, Western patriarchal, phallocratic societies widely enforce upon women minority status. Here is Millett's formulation of the situation: "As the largest alienated element in our society, and because of their numbers, passion, and length of oppression, its largest revolutionary base, women might come to play a leadership part in social revolution" (363). A middle-of-the-road solution to the problems at hand comes with Showalter's framing of white women's literature in post-Enlightenment England as constituting the production of a *subculture* variously aligned with the dominant patriarchal culture, sometimes imitating it, sometimes protesting against it, and sometimes innovating in relation to it. Gilbert and Gubar agree with "Showalter that nineteenth-century literary women *did* have both a literature and a culture of their own" (xii). As I see it, to the extent that white women in Western countries constitute long-standing oppressed subcultures, they are "minorities" and, therefore, any discussion of the pluralizing of poetics should take into account the literary work of these women as a distinct area of inquiry.

Minoritarian Poetics

The pluralizing of poetics follows certain general lines of development. People coming from oppressed groups, colonized collectivities, and ethnic populations produce cultures different from mainstream majority cultures. Specifically, minority literatures exhibit distinctive images, rhythms, characters, themes, structures, genres, and styles. Minority languages are often "dialects" or altogether different (as in the cases of various aboriginal literatures). Even when the minority regimes of reason are thoroughly interwoven with majority regimes, such crossings create third entities—distinctive hybrid regimes. Typically, minorities can either recall or hypothesize a time when the alien hegemonic regime had not yet arrived. One thinks of pre-diaspora Africa or archetypal matriarchal culture. The attraction of such mythicized times may prompt attempts to restore lost values, shuck off the supplementary imposed modes of the majority, return "home," or institute a new homeland. Conversely, some members of minorities may wish to forget the past in order to join the majority; others may want to work in coalitions with the majority without renouncing minority ways and traditions. Numerous sociopolitical permutations are possible. Among those seeking separation, however moderate or extreme, emphasis generally falls on the distinctiveness of minority history and culture. The specific lines of separation may be racial, national, tribal, linguistic, geographical, religious, sexual, class-based, or some combination of these. Essentialisms may emerge, as in the case of Baraka's concept of "blackness" or of Cixous's notion of *écriture féminine* (discussed in chapter 3), promoting such metaphorical notions as pure "blackness" or pure "femininity." Often enough these essentialisms engender or accompany separatist politics, occasionally calling for purges in the name of purification. The temptations here are alluring. Because minority efforts to get free of oppressive dominant regimes in the interest of self-determination are defensive reactions, they are inescapably linked to majority regimes—through opposition. At a minimum, therefore, minority poetics are always at least two-stranded, which is a shorthand way to depict their hybrid intertextuality.

The subject-position structurally characteristic of minorities requires notice here. Despite differences among oppressed groups, the formation of subjectivity among minorities typically involves continuous economic exploitation, racial or sexual or other discrimination, political disenfranchisement, social segregation or marginalization, cultural and psychic denigration, ideological domination, and institutional manipulation. JanMohamed and Lloyd observe that minority subjectivity is "collective" as is most visibly manifested in the fact that "minority individuals are always treated and forced to experience themselves generically" (10). At best the process of becoming-minor is only secondarily a matter of individuation. This is a point broadly illustrated by Harlow in her study of resistance literatures. My argument in chapter 2 about the author as a spokesperson for a group finds special confirmation in the phenomenon of minority subjectivity. Speaking about the subjectivity of insurgent peasants in nineteenth-century India, Spivak observes: "I am progressively inclined, then, to read the retrieval of subaltern consciousness as the charting of what in post-structuralist language would be called the subaltern subject-effect. A subject-effect can be briefly plotted as follows: that which seems to operate as a subject may be part of an immense discontinuous network ('text' in the general sense) of strands that may be termed politics, ideology, economics, history, sexuality, language, and so on" (204). The subject-positions of subalterns spring forth as cultural productions entangled with strands of history characterized by domination and resistance.

Minorities have literatures of their own. As Florence Howe theorizes it, "Art is neither anonymous nor universal; it springs from the particulars of gender as well as class, race, age, and cultural experi-

ence" (190). What typically motivates minority poeticians and critics, therefore, are efforts 1) to specify the biological, psychological,
socioeconomic, historical, political, and/or linguistic shaping forces
on literature; 2) to counter negative majoritarian presuppositions,
images, practices, canons, and institutions; and 3) to recover and
scrutinize denigrated literary works, creating new cultural histories.
By definition, minority criticism depends not only on research and
restoration but resistance. Because such cultural work widely employs
reading as resistance, it should be no surprise that the pluralizing of
poetics engenders cultural critique of the status quo. Put differently,
affirmative theories of minority discourse inescapably entail ethicopolitical stances against domination. Said generalizes the issues for
criticism this way: "Fields of learning, as much as the works of even
the most eccentric artist, are constrained and acted upon by society,
by cultural traditions, by worldly circumstance, and by stabilizing
influences like schools, libraries, and governments" (201). Minority
criticism, like minority poetics, involves opposition across all the registers of hegemonic regimes of reason.

Postcolonial Theory

Among contemporary thinkers perhaps the most influential *locus
classicus* for minoritarian concepts of culture is Fanon's theorizing
about the structure of colonial societies and the need for violent revolution against European colonialism in Africa. I want to examine this
line of thinking, particularly its problematical theories of revolutionary culture. "The colonial world is a Manichean world" (41), proclaims Fanon.

> The Manicheism of the settler produces a Manicheism of the na-
> tive. To the theory of the "absolute evil of the native" the theory of
> the "absolute evil of the settler" replies. The appearance of the set-
> tler has meant in the terms of syncretism the death of the aboriginal
> society, cultural lethargy, and the petrification of individuals. For
> the native, life can only spring up again out of the rotting corpse of
> the settler. This then is the correspondence, term by term, between

the two trains of reasoning. But it so happens that for the colonized people this violence, because it constitutes their only work, invests their characters with positive and creative qualities. (93)

In Fanon's view, decolonization through violent revolution is necessary and valuable as the way to self-determination and nation-building; moreover, in the postcolonial period internecine violence is, again, essential to circumvent the restoration of neocolonial regimes by Europeanized native bourgeoisies. During the phases of such transformations, the arts play various changing roles.

Colonial writers, according to Fanon, progress through three psychopoetic stages: 1) unqualified assimilation of the settlers' literature; 2) prerevolutionary disgust over the colonial present and nostalgia for the native past; and 3) literature of combat calling the masses to awaken and revolt in the name of the coming nation. In addition, the genres of literature alter in phases, as, for example, the drama: "Comedy and farce disappear, or lose their attraction. As for dramatization, it is no longer placed on the plane of the troubled intellectual and his tormented conscience. By losing its characteristics of despair and revolt, the drama becomes part of the common lot of the people and forms part of an action in preparation or already in progress" (241). In revolutionary societies under colonial regimes, all the arts undergo similar alterations, including dance, poetry, music, handicrafts, and storytelling, bearing witness to a rebirth of the imagination.

Fanon puts forward his binary concept of Manicheism, his idea of a three-stage psychopoetics, and his various notions of genre transformations as characteristic of all revolutionary colonial societies in the violent process of nation-building. It is not simply a question of Algeria or Africa at large; modulations are not offered. Fanon universalizes the destinies of all postcolonial nations. He speaks in the name of "peasant" classes and against native bourgeoisies; he advocates nationalism and fulminates against tribalism; he celebrates the countryside against the metropolis. In this context, one can understand his revealing criticism of the pan-African negritude movement, a criticism exhibiting, nevertheless, some sympathy and tolerance:

The concept of negritude, for example, was the emotional if not the logical antithesis of that insult which the white man flung at humanity. This rush of negritude against the white man's contempt showed itself in certain spheres to be the one idea capable of lifting interdictions and anathemas. . . . The unconditional affirmation of African culture has succeeded the unconditional affirmation of European culture. . . .

The poets of negritude will not stop at the limits of the continent. From America, black voices will take up the hymn with fuller unison. (212–13)

Negritude therefore finds its first limitation in the phenomena that take account of the formation of the historical character of men. Negro and African-Negro culture broke up into different entities because the men who wished to incarnate these cultures realized that every culture is first and foremost national, and that the problems which kept Richard Wright or Langston Hughes on the alert were fundamentally different from those which might confront Leopold Senghor or Jomo Kenyatta. (216)

According to Fanon, the negritude movement is, structurally speaking, a reaction formation in line with the imposed Manichean framework of colonial society. It represents only one phase in the awakening of black native intellectuals. But this immature cultural internationalism, nostalgic and defensive, must finally fail in the face of the pressing economic and political specificities of differing national histories and needs. Here, as elsewhere, Fanon's thinking grounds itself thoroughly in the concept of nation in opposition particularly to contending concepts of tribal society, federations of tribes, and international solidarity.

What is perhaps most troubling about such theorizing in the name of the nation is the peculiar status of the so-called nations in modern Africa. From the point of view of precolonial tribal geography, the colonial inscription of "national" boundaries amounts to an arbitrary and fortuitous, alien bureaucratic game of greedy land grabbing. Oddly, Fanon legitimates such unwarranted violent carving, which in a way facilitates the emergence of neocolonial administrations and the continuation of colonial legacies. In poststructuralist terms, Fanon represses historical intertexts—the geographical palimpsests of overlapping borders, populations, and cultural groups—that today return in the form of boundary disputes, linguistic animosities, religious strife, and tribal wars. Paradoxically, it is a question here of Fanon overlooking minorities in the enterprise of nation-building.

In his large-scale study of colonial Anglophone African literature, published two decades after Fanon's work, JanMohamed tellingly declares: "Analysis of the relation between any colonial society and its literature must begin with the fact that the manichean structure of such a society is an economic, social, political, racial, and moral elaboration and distortion of a fundamental ontological opposition between self and other. . . . [The] ideal dialectical relation between self and other is in practice petrified in a colonial situation by the assumed moral superiority of the European which is reinforced at every turn by his actual military supremacy" (264–65). In addition, JanMohamed, like Fanon, in the name of an existential ethics and a realist poetics, judges the concept of negritude to be an imprudent, romanticized valorization of indigenous cultures portraying "an idealized, monolithic, homogenized, and pasteurized 'African' past" (181). To the totalism of the doctrine of negritude JanMohamed opposes the particularism characteristic of each colonial "community." Significantly, JanMohamed avoids the concept of the nation, using instead a vague, undelineated, modest notion of community as well as an unexceptional poetics of realism (derived from Lukács). In the latter instance, to solve the problem of allegorizing inherent in both Manichean societies and in defensive binary doctrines like negritude, JanMohamed relies on traditional mimetic views of literature where present (and future) colonial societies are, by definition, syncretic, many-stranded, contradictory entities. Unlike Fanon, JanMohamed holds to an integrationist sociopolitics without, however, offering any elaboration.

In her evaluation of the theories of colonial discourse constructed by Spivak, Bhabha, and JanMohamed, Parry faults JanMohamed for missing Fanon's subtlety, lacking a utopian dimension, naively crediting authors' intentions, promoting integrationist syncretism, practicing a crude mode of ideological reading, and relying on outmoded mimeticist poetics. The main thrust of this poststructuralist attack is aimed at JanMohamed's existentialist referential manner of construing literary texts, which focuses on surface content and thereby "constrains the examination of the problems inherent in politically heterodox texts working within the structures and redeploying the procedures of modes that naturalize authorized norms and values" (47). What this comes down to is JanMohamed's failure to engage with "the manifold and conflicting textual inscriptions—the discontinuities, defensive rhetorical strategies and unorthodox language challenging official thought, the disruptions of structural unity effected by divergent and discordant voices—as the location and source of the text's politics" (49).

I single out Parry's difficult critique of colonial theory because it usefully focuses on the vexing issue of textual politics, which I want to formulate in poststructuralist terms. The typical modern way of handling the politics of a literary work is, generally speaking, to accord attention and credibility to the statements made by the author and the characters as well as to the outcomes of conflictual plots and characters' destinies. The biography of the author and the sociohistorical context of the work shape the political interpretation of the text in a fairly straightforward manner. Literature reflects life, consciously and unconsciously. Fanon and JanMohamed hold this view. The poststructuralist manner of understanding the politics of a text entails construing the text as a polyvocal discursive fabrication rather than as a monological (or dialogical) intentional representation of a preexisting reality. The system of the text, including particularly its discontinuities, contradictions, parodies, pastiches, figural aberrations, disunities, and discordant voices, produces textual politics. The author may visit the text but only as another voice. History pervades the work in the form of heteroglot intertextual traces refracted and revalued within the text's discursive system. The reticulums of institutions implicated in the production, distribution, and consumption of the text condition the creation and reception of the text, playing a part in, and complicating, its politics.

With regard to the theory of postcolonial discourse, the "Manichean regime" used dramatically by Fanon and JanMohamed names a complex violent intersection of at least two regimes of reason—that of the settlers and that of the natives. Still, the colonial confrontation, broadly construed, say, for all of Africa, involves many tribes and settler nations, many languages and religions, many border disputes and regional usurpations. As a result, "Manicheism" shows itself as mainly a simplified polemical name that designates a structurally binary and hierarchical but semantically empty phenomenon. This religious appellation denotes a violent and fantastical drive for racial purity, separation, and superiority; it does not depict the myriad methods, forms, manifestations, and contradictions of such a drive in practice around the globe. Despite its limitations, the line of postcolonial theory developed by Fanon and extended by JanMohamed forcefully foregrounds the plurality of poetics in the context of cultural domination and "minority" struggles.

The "Minor" and the "Marginal"

At this juncture I want to consider, first, Deleuze and Guattari's eccentric observations about "minor literature" and, second, de Certeau's provocative comments on "marginality." For Deleuze and Guattari the term "minor literature" designates the ubiquitous collective and political utilizations of *major* languages in strange, anarchic, heteroglot ways. Among examples, they surprisingly cite works by Joyce, Artaud, and Kafka, whose inventive and intense employments of major languages, based on hatred of the languages of masters, effect alienations, escapes, and carnivalizations from within, but adjacent to, majoritarian regimes. The main risks run by such minor literatures, according to Deleuze and Guattari, are the temptations to reconstitute power and law, reterritorialize the social field, refashion stable family units, and remake "great literatures." Here it is a matter of revolt turning into reaction. To apply this point to Africa, the solution to white colonial regimes is not, therefore, black neocolonial regimes, but continuous resistance to all regimentation, which resistance, by definition, characterizes the enterprise of a minor literature. In the event that a minor literature weds itself to the dream of a new state, it enters on the path to becoming "great literature," losing its position of adjacency and its vocation of revolt.

If one extended Deleuze and Guattari, one would have to conclude that the politics of existing minority literatures, when linked to projects either of nation-building, equal treatment, or social integration, tend toward regression. One arrives at such a severe judgment on the basis of Deleuze and Guattari's anarchist ethic committed to decentralized communal modes of existence without overarching state apparatuses. In the past such utopian communitarian programs have not appealed to large numbers of oppressed, impoverished, and aggrieved minority subjects. The main problem with Deleuze and Guattari's peculiar definition of "minor literature" is its disembodied "metaphysical" nature. It has nothing specifically to do with racial, sexual, economic, or social discriminations nor with imperialist, colonialist, or patriarchal oppressions. Rather, it describes a perennial politico-aesthetic option in relation to every ruling regime— continuous anti-authoritarian revolt through inventive linguistic means. "Minor literature" becomes a universal function. It does not help matters that Deleuze and Guattari refuse to argue the merits of their (unspoken) major premise that anarchism constitutes a desirable politics for the modern world.

In grappling with the complexities of the concept of "minority," the observations on "marginality" by de Certeau add yet other pertinent complications. "Marginality is today no longer limited to minority groups, but is rather massive and pervasive; this cultural activity of the non-producers of culture, an activity that is unsigned, unreadable, and unsymbolized, remains the only one possible for all those who nevertheless buy and pay for the showy products through which a productivist economy articulates itself. Marginality is becoming universal" (xvii). The gist of de Certeau's argument is that an expanding market economy and technical rationality cast majorities of people into passive consumers in a global system that more and more values certain limited types of production. Increasingly, the majority finds itself in the structural position of immigrant minorities—peoples whose cultural activities are neither regarded nor registered by the reigning regime. De Certeau's particular project is to study the artistic ways of operating—the cultural tactics of everyday life—which are currently unsigned, unreadable, unsymbolized. His thesis is that the quotidian practices of consumers, ranging from shopping, talking, and reading to rhetorical tricks, clever gambits, and simulations, constitute a valuable, hedonistic, inventive art of life. What motivates de Certeau is, in large part, admiration for "minority" cultural tactics.

The obvious weakness of de Certeau's claim is that it collapses the neighboring phenomena of marginalization and minoritization, making them improbably applicable to broad numbers of, among others, Western bourgeois peoples. Ultimately, de Certeau champions creative and pleasurable quotidian practices on too wide a scale. Disenchanted with revolution, he doggedly promotes small-scale and modest resistances across the many facets of an emerging global hegemonic regime of reason. In the present context, perhaps the virtue of de Certeau's thinking is that it suggestively pictures the expanding technocratic market economy as an imperialistic apparatus, casting increasing segments of the world population in positions similar to minorities. This dystopian portrait of collective domination, however, improbably presents "minorities" free of oppressive discrimination and exploitation and furnished with the political franchise. While minorities and majorities may share experiences of marginalization, there is much that they do not share, as, for example, racial or sexual or class discrimination, political disenfranchisement, economic exploitation often approximating slavery, and culturally sanctioned social segregation. Marginalization and minoritization seem altogether different phenomena. Where Deleuze and Guattari equate minority with anarchy, de Certeau links minoritization with marginalization. However suggestive both operations may be, they have the effect of unduly generalizing and desubstantializing the devastating social, economic, political, and racial oppressions experienced by minority cultures.

Pluralizing Poetics and Beyond

The literatures of certain peoples of color, women, colonized populations, and other "minorities" often are, and have been, systematically excluded, denigrated, or ignored by spokespersons for the "great traditions" and by many mainstream literary academics. Such literatures are frequently left to anthropologists, folklorists, and specialists in popular culture. The ethicopolitics at work here effects variations on "to the victors go the spoils" and "only the strong survive." Such a stance is violent, patriarchal, repressive. It is not a simpering piety but a committed inclusivist politics of culture that repudiates this stance that damages many of us each day it continues uncontested. Considered globally, the traditional aestheticist dogma with its hierarchy of genres and its limited framework of canonical touchstones seems a narrow and provincial matter incapable of improvement to meet current circumstances. There are many poetics, not one. The literary epic is a consummate genre only for some few peoples, not all. The same goes for tragic drama and other prized aristocratic European forms.

The pluralizing of poetics, enacted by black aestheticians, feminists, postcolonial theorists, and others, has been going on for several generations and is still going on. Although it has had a growing impact on the academy, literary study, and poetic theory, there is yet a long way to go. In trying to construct an effective mode of cultural analysis reflective of present circumstances, I find the phenomenon of pluralizing poetics basic to any conceptualization of literature(s). Significantly, the model of poetics here is rhizomatous, not arborescent: it is not a question with either "general literature" or with national literatures of a major trunk and minor branches, but of horizontal networks variously intersecting. What constitutes "literature" in one time and place need not resemble that of another period and location.

Literatures proliferate and differ. Of course, they are often harnessed to ambitious political and cultural programs like pacification, acculturation, nationalism, or imperialism, whereupon exclusionary and hierarchical tree diagrams come into play. Major literatures are made, not born.

There is one crucial matter I want to consider in concluding this chapter. The tactic of pluralizing poetics risks recapitulating in a different register the Manichean operation, that is, the pluralizing of poetics responds in a predictable compensatory binary fashion to the existence of hegemonic major literatures. It would be better hereafter to talk differentially of the "pluralizings" of poetics: to pluralize minority poetics in this way is to avoid collapsing all minority literatures into one homogeneous class. It is preposterous to picture as some kind of unified entity all literatures produced by blacks, women, colonial peoples, aboriginals, and so on. In an ideal world it would be possible to talk plurally of literatures and of poetics—of differences without dominations.

6

"Reading" Texts

The work of academic criticism involves such varied tasks as critique, evaluation, exegesis, explication, institutional analysis, interpretation, reception, appreciation, and response. All of these activities generally presuppose well-edited texts as well as linguistic, cultural, and literary competence. Some of these labors of criticism presuppose, furthermore, readers possessing special aesthetic sensitivities, or holding values potentially in conflict with other values, or occupying specific sociohistorical sites. The literacy required of academic criticism depends on conventions, codes, and practices increasingly in dispute in our time. The uncertain destiny of "reading," the polyvalent term here designating the multiple tasks of criticism, creates conditions favorable for reconsidering past critical theories and for developing new perspectives on protocols for reading. In this chapter I shall assess certain conceptualizations of reading, specifically various influential formulations propounded by New Critics, hermeneuticists, structuralists, reader-response theorists, phenomenologists, materialists, and poststructuralists.

Prevailing practices of academic reading continue to stress critical submissiveness, impersonality, and devotion to the "text" narrowly construed. Teachers rarely condone any explicit assessment of values, ideologies, and institutions, nor do they encourage questioning processes of text selection and evaluation. If one wishes to adhere to current pedagogical norms of reading, one must learn to minimize "personal" involvements, to respect the genius of authors, to orchestrate textual implications, figural aberrations, and thematic incongruities, to tie up textual loose ends, to (re)read until critical scrutiny becomes all-seeing and the text iconic, to nod occasionally in the direction of sociohistorical "contexts," to construct coherent documented thesis + proof critical essays, and to call all this activity "*critical* reading." What is perhaps most lacking in this reading formation is anything particularly "critical" in the senses of skeptical, resistant, oppositional. The image of the model reader promotes abnegation of self, admiration for distanced authors, devotion to economically structured complex texts, and minimal attention to social institutions and regimes of reason. We should perhaps stop calling such dutiful and refined textual tinkering "criticism."

Disorders of Reading

Among the more memorable protocols of reading theorized by the New Critics at their most severe are the strictures against both genetic and receptionist approaches, leading to the doctrines condemning the intentional and affective fallacies. The literary text is ideally separated from the gross body of social life and the personal lives of author and reader. Multiple retrospective readings seek to demonstrate the intricate and complex spatial form of individual well-wrought autonomous artifacts whose manifold conflicting forces and incongruities are interrelated and balanced by such metaphorical devices as paradox, ambiguity, and irony. The "meaning" of the text consists not in paraphrasable content nor in extractable propositions but in harmonized connotations, tones, images, symbols, and other semantic features intrinsic to the text. For New Critical formalists, reading entails impersonal and close explication of depersonalized and objectified poetic texts, which through critical labor exhibit complex semantic equilibrium and internal purposiveness. Given the high value assigned poetic complexity, the more incongruities harmonized the more estimable the critical operation.

What is remarkable about this theory of reading is that it programmatically rules out or ignores so much, including considerations of personal response and sociohistorical reception, institutional analysis and ethicopolitical critique, and interpretation of "significance" and "meaning." In this reductive operation, impersonality becomes all-pervasive and doctrinaire. Authors and readers are sacrificed to the glory of the freestanding, monumentalized text. The social body is purged in a manner similar to an ascetical theology contemptuous of the world. In addition, the temporal experience of reading is overcome through repetitive rereadings with the result that texts appear not only iconic and spatial, but also multivalent and intricate in their all-at-onceness. Such panoptical reading seems omniscient, as it is meant to. Long diffusive genres cannot compete well with brief dense works. A premium is placed on achieved balance, harmony, and unity, purchased by subduing discontinuities, contradictions, and gaps through (re)coding them as paradoxes, ironies, and ambiguities. Constrained, hollowed out, and aestheticized, "meaning" becomes insubstantial for fear that literature may otherwise compete with religion, morality, philosophy, law, science, politics, all of which it must transcend. The result of such reduction is that criticism functions primarily as adulation; opposition and resistance find little place. Furthermore, one can neither legitimately play with the centrifugal elements of the text nor poach on it for pleasure or knowledge. New Critical "reading" appears repressed, defensive, obsessional. What such reading can, nevertheless, contribute to poststructuralist cultural criticism is a penchant for explication sensitive to textual complexities and incongruities reconstrued in this new enterprise as material not for rhetorical harmonization but for deconstruction and symptomal assessment.

The philological effort of Hirsch to counter the New Critics' taboos on auctorial intention, reader's response, and historical criticism is at once salutary and problematic. In Hirsch's hermeneutical theory, texts have meaning as a consequence of authors' intentions, which, however, are public not private and which must be validated using tests of probability. Moreover, the intention, embodied in the text, stabilizes for all time the meaning. The main task of interpretation is antiquarian reconstruction of auctorial intention in line with verifiable textual details and norms of historical horizons. In addition to such historical regularities, conventions of genre serve as constraints in the labor of interpretation. The associations, interests, and values that texts may possess for individual contemporary readers constitute its "significance" (not "meaning"), which "criticism" (not "interpretation" proper) works to specify. Significance is variable; meaning is stable. Criticism is subjective; interpretation is objective. The former deals with values and the latter with facts. The one admits readers' responses and the other credits authors' intentions. For Hirsch the primary endeavor of literary analysis is indisputably interpretation, not criticism.

The whole theory of reading erected by Hirsch depends on extensive elaborations wrought on the dubious binary split between "public/private" where the first term systematically receives privileged status. The main task of literary analysis is interpretation rather than criticism—exegesis dominates over evaluation and cultural critique. Horizons and genres, regularized public constructs, effectively circumscribe biographical inquiry and intertextual research. Purportedly, what is public is both stable and determinate and what is private is both fluid and indeterminate. In spite of his obsessions with the public and the stable, Hirsch portrays "interpretation" as a two-stage process that moves from intuitive divinatory identification to intellectual interpretation proper. The job of the critic is to submit the prereflective reenactment of the text to a "severe discipline" (x) of reflective reconstruction employing tests of verification and standards of probability. The nexus of notions here reduces to a set of disturbing wishful dictums: suppress the subjective, overcome blind spots and prejudices, subordinate values, constrain fluidity, insure correctness, promote discipline. In light of such ideas, it is no surprise that Hirsch ends up championing typed authors and hegemonic horizons, ignoring the eccentric, the marginal, the resistant.

To elaborate on a key point broached here and in several earlier chapters, the reading of a text from the outset often involves, more or less simultaneously, appreciation, critique, exegesis, evaluation, explication, institutional analysis, reception, and response. None of these activities need wait upon the completion of the others or of the text. It is true that university literature students frequently encounter sequential assignments, moving from, say, textual explication to personal response to evaluation, which suggest that the activity of explication necessarily and logically precedes response and evaluation. Pedagogical systematization, habitual and normative, creates false impressions and questionable modes of reading. It would not be uncommon for a reader, for example, a resisting minority reader, to initiate a critique and institutional analysis after responding to only several pages of a novel. The reader may find both the plot and the imagery portraying a female character highly insulting. Thereupon may follow preliminary consideration of the publisher, place and date of publication, dedication, author's reputation, dustjacket promotion, and design of the bookjacket, all seeking to situate the work in some intersection of networks of institutions and regimes of reason. The key point is that the first principle of reading is not selfless, disinterested, detached explication or exegesis followed by personal, interested, activist response, or appreciation, or evaluation, or critique. Reading does not progress from the impersonal to the personal, from the public to the private, from the neutral to the ideological. Nor, on the other hand, is the first principle of reading a subjective, intuitive response, appreciation, or reception followed by an objective, intellectual explication, exegesis, or interpretation.

In depicting reading as a process that progresses from identification to interpretation to criticism, Hirsch promotes impersonal exegesis over (unavoidable) response and (optional) critique. What results from this fictitious account of reading is celebration of the text and sacrifice of the critic's self. As employed in Hirsch's philological hermeneutics, the special concepts "meaning"/"significance," "interpretation"/"criticism," and "intention"/"horizon" function regressively, reenforcing the practices of poet worship, idolatry of the text, monological genre pragmatics, subordination of the reader, and devotion to textual coherence.

The theories of reading developed by Booth, Scholes, and Miller, discussed in chapter 1, exhibit similar problems when construing the phenomenology of reading. To recapitulate, Booth approves of ethical critique (so-called overstanding) provided it is preceded by "understanding"—as though such a sequence were inevitable. But as one reads a text, critique may emerge to form the "basis" of understanding. Booth misconstrues reading not only in his explanation of understanding/overstanding, but in his treatment of "understanding" as a universal norm. Contending interpretive communities undermine this value. Scholes's special version of "reading," "interpretation," and "criticism"—roughly explication, exegesis, cultural critique—misleadingly implies that these three activities occur sequentially in separate zones involving distinct operations. His ruminations in *Protocols of Reading* and *Textual Power* solidify the impression that critique constitutes the culmination and endpoint of critical effort rather than, say, a point of departure or a general aspect of reading. Like Hirsch and Booth, Scholes presents critique as optional, though Booth and Scholes both wish to increase its use among students and professors. For Scholes an unnamed, preliminary phase of critical activity, seemingly prior to explication, engenders "bewilderment" from which the reader must get free in order to move reading toward criticism. What characterizes the various phases of reading is a progressive separation, going from fascinated and dutiful immersion in textual details and exegetical enigmas to distanced assessment of themes and codes undertaken on behalf of a group. Interestingly, critique requires the exertion of collective or class interests and values against the interests and values of the text and against the bewilderment experienced by the individual reader. The subjectivity of the reader is simultaneously socialized and individualized. In the end, Scholes depicts reading as progressing from private to public, resembling Miller in this regard. Distinguishing between "reading" and "criticism," Miller casts the former as a "private" and inaugurating, ethicolinguistic phenomenon that inescapably leads to the latter public activity, manifested in print and classroom dialogue and engaged with politics, history, epistemology, and social institutions. First there is reading and then criticism; the private precedes the public. Oddly, the "private" is here primordial and prepsychological, linked with linguistic determinism and its inescapable errancy. Thus "reading" (or rather "misreading") improbably takes place uncontaminated by (personal) interests, prejudices, values, or blind spots. It is a question of linguistic destiny shaping subjectivity on its way to entering social space. This special sequential version of critical activity repeats disorders common to many contemporary theories of reading, particularly in its skirting of critique.

In my view, the reading of texts depends, in large measure, on acquired linguistic, cultural, and literary conventions and practices. Reading texts is an activity inescapably entangled with syntax, grammar, tropology, epistemology, ethics, psychology, history, economics, politics, literary history, and social institutions with no sure way of assigning fixed priorities. An indispensable dimension of reading is the subjectivity of the reader—an ongoing process shaped by entries into and engagements with language and the social order, which themselves involve changing placements of the body, changing formations of consciousness, and changing interpellations in regimes of reason. In my formulation, the reader "possesses" both public and private facets of "being" with no guaranteed procedures for neatly separating these dimensions. Thus to conceive reading as a serial operation composed of discrete stages which progress from personal to public matters or vice versa is to create an impoverished linear pedagogical model misleading in its fabricated analytical simplicity. Reading is, to a considerable extent, a regimented activity. As with all regimens, the protocols for reading can be more or less severe, more or less life-enhancing, more or less restrictive. The limited subject-positions regularly assigned to readers strike me as faulty and dangerous primarily because a premium is put on submission, obedience, and puzzle solving, rather than on resistance and self-determination. What disturbs me about the staging of reading as a process going from private to public engagements or from public to private ones is the resulting (non)status of critique in relation to other tasks of reading. It is "ideological," in the bad sense of the word, to render cultural critique out of place, optional, supplementary, tertiary, or epiphenomenal. To fulfill with subtlety and energy dutiful service functions of literary criticism is not enough. To repress cultural critique is too much.

The Matter of Evaluation

The practice of evaluation is an aspect of criticism long marginalized among academic intellectuals. It is, to begin with, frequently forgotten that writing itself involves continuous acts of judgment in the selection and shaping of words, phrases, images, figures, etc. The resultant myriad acts of approval and disapproval are not simply personal, given that various audiences and institutions put pressures on authors and create feedback effects. Moreover, unconscious elements in such transactions permeate the flows of judgments. Similarly, the process of reading a text prompts numerous evaluative responses affected, consciously and unconsciously, by various audiences and institutions. As a result, evaluation is multilayered, continuous, communal-personal, institutional, contingent. Institutional agents enmeshed in evaluative activities include editors, publishers, readers, reviewers, distributors, bookstore owners, libraries, teachers, students, anthologists, translators, awards judges, scholars, reprinters, imitators, and so on. Let me exaggerate to make several points—the time of evaluation is always; the place is everywhere; the modes are legion, ranging from coded grins and constructed image clusters at micro levels to "impartial" monographs and outraged moral condemnations at macro levels. There is no escaping evaluation, though certain modes are usually preferred over others.

An obvious precondition of academic forms of evaluation is the existence of culturally "competent" and "literate" readers situated amid institutions and regimes of reason. At whatever time and place and under whatever particular conditions, evaluators occupy specific sites, which is to say that not only cultural knowledge and skill but personal interests and prejudices constitute conditions of possibility for academic evaluation. Barbara Herrnstein Smith dramatizes such contingency of value by observing that "no matter how magisterially delivered and with what attendant claims or convictions of universality, unconditionality, impersonality, or objectivity, any assertion of '*the* value' of some object can always be unpacked as a judgment of its *contingent* value and appropriated accordingly" (97). The target of this observation is traditional axiology with its wishful claim to objective and universal validity for its evaluative standards and judgments. Evaluators are implicated in regimes of reason, which accounts to some extent for both the variability and the stability of cultural judgments. Also membership in interpretive communities helps explain evaluative agreements and disputes. And personal libidinal styles of investment, though unconsciously at work, produce certain stabilities and instabilities in the process of evaluation. Ultimately, the contingency of value makes it inevitable that the multifaceted evaluative judgments involved in response, exegesis, institutional analysis, and critique are partial and conflictual. To read is to take stands, however much such positionings may be habitual, unconscious, or "automatic."

Problems with Reader-Response Theories

In specifying the numerous codes and conventions of literary interpretation, structuralists concerned with reader reception usefully illustrate the tacit public-private knowledge constituting reading regimens and practices. Among many codes and conventions, Culler, for example, isolates the following six (115–16). The "rule of significance" dictates that a literary work expresses a significant attitude about man or the world. The "convention of metaphorical coherence" states that metaphorical tenors and vehicles are always coherent. The "code of poetic tradition" provides a stock of symbols and types with agreed-upon meanings. The "convention of genre" offers stable sets of norms against which to assess texts. The "convention of thematic unity" declares that semantic and figurative oppositions fit into symmetrical binary patterns. And the "rule of totality" requires works to be coherent on as many levels as possible. In the event that authors engage in convention-breaking, the reader understands such procedures in the context of stable conventions. Moreover, textual gaps emerge as such in relation to expectations of totality. The rules of grammar explain phenomena of ungrammaticality. From this influential perspective, the main drive of critical reading is to render literary texts completely communicative: "The strange, the formal, the fictional, must be recuperated or naturalized" (134), states Culler in describing the structuralist account of reader response.

There are problems with the structuralist project, though I shall forgo rehearsing the well-known broad poststructuralist critique of structuralism. Let me single out a few key items related to theory of reader response. According to structuralists, protocols of reading facilitate total interpretation. In the best of cases, readers would possess complete mastery of codes, conventions, and practices, which is why Culler speaks of "ideal readers" and Riffaterre of "superreaders." What is at issue in structuralist theorizing about readers is neither the subjectivity nor experience nor skill of "real" readers, but the maximal systematic competence of hypothetical model readers. Nothing presumably escapes the superreader armed with consummate competence capable of rendering any textual ungrammaticality meaningful. The mission is total communication through complete naturalization. The poststructural theory of "misreading," to be discussed shortly, runs counter to almost every element of this formula for reading, particularly its array of impossible commitments to hyperhermeneutic mastery, competence, communication, naturalization, unification, "grammatization," and totalization. Many of the conventions isolated and dignified by structuralists are contested by poststructuralists, as, for example, the conventions of thematic unity, metaphorical coherence, and generic norms. Mastery of texts using such interpretive and evaluative instruments amounts to storytelling, which is how Culler later characterizes such reading in *On Deconstruction,* where he distances himself from structuralism.

There are several aspects of Bleich's early subjectivist theory of reader response that merit attention in the present context. On the negative side, Bleich fatally models reading for explicit pedagogical reasons as a process going from authentic private response to falsifying public interpretation. On the positive side, he takes into consideration, as part of reading, both unavoidable psychological "distortions" and certain institutional requirements of the discipline. "Distortion" in psychological terminology does not, of course, imply the possibility of correction: unconscious processes of condensation, displacement, symbolization, secondary revision, and defense shape materials in particular ways, which subjects are not free to control. In Bleich's view, the reading of a text bears the marks of revealing and valuable distortions, namely associations, exaggerations, omissions, insertions, and "errors." These constitute evidence of intense engagement with the text. What Bleich deplores is any attempt to erase or rule out such predetermining psychological "idiosyncrasies" in the name of objectivity, completeness, or discipline. In addition, Bleich criticizes the institutional requirements that readings be packaged in critical essays presenting proposition-proof arguments—which function to extinguish eccentricities and "distortions." Here Bleich touches on an issue memorably developed by Hartman who argues affirmatively for creative modes of critical writing exceeding the normative academic essay/article. Because I credit the "subjectivity" of the reader in the project of cultural criticism, I find Bleich helpful in theorizing the "distortions" of the reader. To these I would add other types of misprisions, as we shall see a bit later. For Bleich reading emerges as "misreading" with no uncoercive way to "cure" the situation so as to insure uniformity of response. Reigning disciplinary protocols normalize and falsify reading in the interest of an ersatz uniformity. What I wish to contest in my account of reading is the installation of bewildered, bodiless, submissive, blank readers who seek to serve as authors' or personas' ventriloquists. That is why the work of oppositional minority readers and the phenomenon of distortion are important, for they evidence resisting bodies/subjects possessing desires, interests, and values that shape reading.

The significant issue of the temporality of reading deserves consideration in this discussion. Against the retrospective, objectified, and spatialized readings sought by formalists and structuralists, various phenomenologists, hermeneuticists, and reader-response critics advocate dialogical encounters with texts, focused on the unfolding process of reading as it happens. Reading undergoes a slow-motion operation, becoming risky event, act, performance, opening to view affective and didactic potentialities. Such attention to response and reception casts "interpretation" not as a labor of textual verification or of methodological cross-examination, but of exploration capable of transforming readers. In this atomizing view of reading, textual form appears as retrospective construction, enforcing totalizing closure; if there is to be "form," it should be serial, sequential, temporal.

The general problem with the suggestive phenomenological theory of reader response is its failure to credit the polyvalent processes and many dimensions of reading. To conceive reading as essentially the conjuncture of consciousness and temporality is to overlook a great deal. The primordial scene of reading in this scenario risks excluding considerations of, for example, the determining codes and conventions of "literacy," the distortions of the unconscious, the many shaping forms of regimes of reason on authors and readers, and the practices of hostile oppositional reading. The reader emerges peculiarly as an unspecific private disembodied consciousness serving general ontological functions. There is no public sphere to speak of. Preoccupation and identification with the unfolding text tend to suppress, if not rule out, taking stances against the text. Institutions like schools, families, churches, and worksites appear nonexistent. The phenomenological procedures of bracketing and reduction end up rendering literary discourse a mode of "authentic speech" of a singularly purified sort, seemingly uncomplicated by disabling linguistic aberrations and labyrinthine intertextual implications. In this work of reading, the act of linking together phrases generates wonder and insight, not social and political struggle as Lyotard persuasively portrays it. What a phenomenological theory of reading as process can, nevertheless, add to poststructuralist criticism is an understanding of reading as a complex performance holding potentially high stakes for the reader. One message is texts shape lives. Another lesson is that the phenomenon of temporality disrupts the practice of spatializing. More on this point follows.

Theory of reader response continues to be galvanized by Fish's concept of "interpretive communities," a notion at once helpful and wanting. According to Fish, "interpretive communities are made up of those who share interpretive strategies not for reading (in the conventional sense) but for writing texts, for constituting their properties and assigning their intentions. In other words, these strategies exist prior to the act of reading and therefore determine the shape of what is read rather than, as is usually assumed, the other way around"(171). Each community of interpreters deciphers texts in the manner directed by its interpretive strategies. Because readers can belong to several communities, their interpretations can vary. Fish gives us communal readers predisposed to create particular meanings and, in doing so, he helpfully opens to view questions about rewriting protocols, institutional groupings, the politics of interpretation, and the mechanisms of professionalism. At the same time he breaks up the totalizing structuralist account of reading conventions. It is clear that Fish regards rationality as community-based and critical inquiry as contingent. Readers do not transcend beliefs, interests, assumptions, points of view, and allegiances; they are situated in highly specific ways.

The hostile secondary literature generated by Fish's theory of reading is too extensive to examine here. Among those associated with various modes of materialist criticism, I find useful the objections lodged by Cain, Eagleton, Lentricchia, Mailloux, Pratt, and Said, all of whom characterize Fish's theory as wanting in similar ways. Let me list some salient limitations drawn from Fish's critics and from my own reflections. Fish stops short of analyzing the sociopolitics of interpretive communities; his literary readers exhibit subjectivities undetermined by broad ethnic, social, and political forces; he walls off professional communities from historical processes and social structures; he avoids ideological analysis of all kinds; he pictures interpretive communities too idealistically as free from disagreements, conflicts, and power struggles; he installs "consensus" as the outcome of communal labor; he relativizes the relations among groups in the name of an overly cheerful equality, fraternity, and freedom; he promotes a consumerist view of literature inattentive to problems of cultural production and of authorship; he restricts institutional analysis largely to professional disciplinary matters; he does not adequately take into account such phenomena as distortion, contradiction, and unreadability; he minimizes the operation of cross-communal hegemonic strategies of reading; and he unrealistically renders reading protocols as at once a matter of free choice and willing submission. The thrust of such criticism points up several general areas of weakness. Fish downplays the complexities involved in the production, distribution, and maintenance of literature, and he simplifies the intricacies, particularly the agonistic features, of subjectivity and community membership. Fish disregards many of the effects of regimes of reason. What his view comes down to at its simplest is: a text is what any homogeneous group freely decides to make of it.

In spite of its limitations, work on reader response benefits theory of reading in several important ways. It undermines any simple notion of "right" reading and any idea of reading as mechanistic scanning or decoding. The subjectivities of readers and the stability of texts become problematic thanks to reception theory. Renewed attention to the moment-by-moment activities of reading and to institutional norms of literacy complicate hermeneutical concepts of time and history, of self and community. Finally, response theory shows reading to be a mode of writing inherently differential and appropriative, an avenue of inquiry fruitfully pursued by "poststructuralists" like Bloom and Jameson, as we shall see.

Two Modes of Misreading

The theory of literary reading as misreading, developed by de Man and reconfigured by Bloom, challenges contending accounts of reading primarily on the basis of language theory. In an essay critical of Fish and others, de Man declares that "the determining characteristic of literary language is indeed figurality, in the somewhat wider sense of rhetoricity, but that, far from constituting an objective basis for literary study, rhetoric implies the persistent threat of misreading"

(*BI*, 285) and, more pointedly, "the specificity of literary language resides in the possibility of misreading and misinterpretation" (280). As discussed in chapter 3, de Man equates degrees of literariness with degrees of rhetoricity. The figurality of a literary text produces referential aberrations, rendering critical misprision inescapable. Given that literary "reading" engenders misreading, it is not too surprising that de Man distinguishes between good and bad misreadings. By definition, a good misreading creates a text that itself begets a misreading and so on in a productive series. Like critics, authors misread their own texts. The "fault" lies not with readers but with language. In narrating disorienting reading experiences, critical writing itself relies on figural language, creating "allegories of reading." In other words, criticism cannot simply describe, repeat, or represent a text because no unrhetorical or scientific, transcendental metalanguage exists. And even the most scrupulous paraphrase blurs textual aberrations in the forced homogeneities of its own allegorizing rendition of (mis)reading. Finally, texts, according to de Man, misread themselves regardless of critics' and authors' intentions: "A literary text simultaneously asserts and denies the authority of its own rhetorical mode" (*AR*, 17).

It goes without saying that de Man's theory of misreading does not put an end to critical reading and writing; it does, however, undermine many of the claims made for reading by other critical theorists. The various reading protocols of formalists, structuralists, and hermeneuticists that direct critics, for example, to harmonize textual elements, establish metaphorical coherence, unify thematic materials, totalize as many textual levels as possible, achieve maximum communication, and link meaning to auctorial intention appear dubious in light of de Man's theorizing. In de Man's account, reading characteristically confronts undecidable textual discontinuities, incoherencies, disunities, and incompatibilities on account of figural oscillations and ungrammaticalities, which frustrate interpretative competence and mastery, thoroughly compromising referentiality and communication. Reading faces vertiginous possibilities of aberration.

The outcome of de Man's theorizing is to render the reader dizzy to the point of submissiveness, demanding Sisyphean effort just to mount a (mis)reading and according no space to ethicopolitical resistance and critique. Where Lyotard construes the activity of linking phrases in forming an interpretation as inaugurating social and political forces, de Man characterizes such labor as composing fictions out of randomness. For de Man reading remains permanently stalled in exegetical puzzling. All else goes largely unattended. It is, therefore, not surprising that Lentricchia faults de Man for avoiding the fact that rhetoric is a primary agency of social action and change, playing a leading role in maintaining and perpetuating dominant ideology. Texts constitute and shape lives and social arrangements. While insisting on the persuasive powers of rhetoric, however, Lentricchia glides too quickly over the problematics of figural duplicity. In my view, a more incisive criticism of de Man concerns his singular avoidance of intertextuality and heteroglossia, both of which connect text to social text and institutions including regimes of reason. De Man ignores the communal aspects of textual rhetoric and reading, being preoccupied with figural enigmas and their (mis)reading. The hyperbolic charge that de Man's theory of reading institutes a new New Criticism is partially justified.

The theory of misreading, as developed by de Man, retains the New Critical taboos against intentionalism and affectivism. Agency is suppressed by de Man who exhibits little interest in the subjectivities of either authors or readers. The forces of the unconscious and the body are outside de Man's evident concerns. One has to turn to Bloom for a theory of misreading attentive to the question of subjectivity, only in this case it is the subjectivity of anxious newcomer authors, not critical readers, that is primarily at issue.

Bloom tellingly observes in *The Anxiety of Influence* that "poets' misinterpretations or poems are more drastic than critics' misinterpretations or criticism, but this is only a difference in degree and not at all in kind. There are no interpretations but only misinterpretations" (94–95). Extending Bloom's observation, one arrives at a conceptualization of critical reading as an activity in which repetition of and identification with a canonical poetic text are impossible. Such ideals are, in any event, slavish and deadening. In order defensively to insure his own survival, independence, and triumph, the strong critic unconsciously represses the powerful precursor text, opening a space for creative misprision facilitated by rhetorical troping. Critical "distortion" is both psychological and rhetorical—in that order. The vigorous (mis)reading of a text requires aggression and self-assertion, which makes clear that Bloomian misreading occurs not because of inescapable linguistic slippage but because of necessary psychological defense manifesting itself in rhetorical aberration.

As portrayed by Bloom, the strong misreading subject is competitive, vengeful, driven, isolated. Just how much the threatened will comes into play is unclear, though the critical will-to-power appears considerable. In any event, the unconscious generates misreading. Parenthetically, Bloom continues the tradition of bardolatry with his blanket dictum that poets' misreadings are more drastic than critics'. When they come to revise Bloom in their feminist theorizing about "anxiety of authorship," Gilbert and Gubar depict the inferiority of feminine subjectivity as socially constructed. Similarly, JanMohamed presents the enforced generic identity of colonized subjects as culturally imposed. Bloom's version of subjectivity conflicts with minority accounts, pitting an isolated and disembodied "presocial" unconscious against a communally shaped psyche. If there is a "community" for Bloom, it is composed of two highly individualistic antagonists— the precursor and the ephebe. Minor figures remain irrelevant. As a result, reading is resistance for Bloom, but such resistance always occurs one-on-one between heroic combatants. Criticism as either cultural critique or institutional analysis is out of place in this grimly reductive scenario. Critics and poets display extremely limited links to regimes of reason, which are largely restricted in Bloom to a few interrelated literary masterpieces taken quietly out of the broader cultural intertext. Bloom overlooks the formation of required linguistic, social, and literary skills and conventions needed to empower the reading and writing of poetry. The ethicopolitics of culture at work here can be formulated this way: the legacies of the meek are the triumphs of the strong.

Reading as Allegorical Rewriting

At this point I want to scrutinize the theory of reading developed by Jameson in *The Political Unconscious*, which is antithetical to much of the theorizing examined thus far in this chapter. In *Marxism and Form*, Jameson had promoted an existentialist mode of Marxist dialectical criticism that moved self-consciously from analysis of the private artwork of individual consciousness to the public reality of collective history, calling the shift of levels and moment of linkage "totalization," the task of which was "to reconcile the inner and the outer, the intrinsic and extrinsic, the existential and the historical" (330–31). This early formulation, scrapped in *The Political Unconscious*, rests on a private/public polarity that divides existence into two separable realms, conceiving reading as a sequential progression from one sphere to the other: reading closes the rift and "materializes" consciousness, joining the aesthetic and the social. The later conceptualization of Marxist cultural criticism singles out three semantic horizons construed as progressively wider concentric frameworks of analysis.

The first horizon of interpretation in Jameson's scheme treats the text as a symbolic act that offers imaginary resolutions of real sociopolitical contradictions. (There is no initial privatization of the text here.) Derived from the work of Lévi-Strauss and Greimas, such interpretative inquiry explicitly casts the aesthetic work as political endeavor. The second horizon examines the text as an utterance (*parole*) of antagonistic dialogical class discourses (*langue*). Inspired by Bakhtin, this frame of analysis seeks to foreground and revalue oppositional voices as well as hegemonic ones, picturing the text as a heteroglot social document. The third horizon studies the text as a specific conjuncture that recalls and projects all the conflicting historical modes of production. Indebted to the work of Poulantzas, this horizon depicts cultural existence as in perpetual "revolution" where coexisting modes of production clash so that the intertextual aesthetic text manifests history in a broad yet special sense. Each of the three operations of criticism, according to Jameson, entails allegorical interpretive rewriting of the text using three coded frameworks. In addition, "a Marxist negative hermeneutic, a Marxist practice of ideological analysis proper, must in the practical work of reading and interpretation be exercised *simultaneously* with a Marxist positive hermeneutic, or a decipherment of the Utopian impulses of these same still ideological cultural texts" (296).

There are serious drawbacks to Jameson's ambitious project for reading. While he helpfully characterizes the text as both heteroglot and intertextual, he explicitly restricts such conceptions to orthodox Marxian notions. The heteroglossia of the text, to start with, is firmly joined to and limited by Marxian class theory: "For Marxism classes must always be apprehended relationally, and . . . the ultimate (or ideal) form of class relationship and class struggle is always dichotomous. The constitutive form of class relationships is always that between a dominant and a laboring class. . . . To define class in this way is sharply to differentiate the Marxian model of classes from the conventional sociological analysis of society into strata, subgroups, professional elites and the like" (83–84). The point is the heteroglossia of the text "must" "always" exhibit antagonistic relations between classes and class factions: dedication to the labor metaphysic and to the proletariat motivates this narrowed version of heteroglossia. The result is that the second horizon of interpretation is allegorical in a highly special, prescriptive sense. Analogously, the historical "intertextuality" of the artwork "must" "always" be rewritten in terms of the Marxian theory of successive and overlapping modes of production, rendering the third horizon of interpretation an operation of equally prescriptive allegorizing. Social history manifests a teleological progression, complete with temporary regressions, from tribal societies to hierarchical kinship societies to despotism to oligarchical slaveholding societies to feudalism, capitalism, and socialism/communism. While the idea that these modes of production coexist in any one historical conjuncture enriches the enterprise of

Marxist historical interpretation, it ties such reading to a dubious deterministic account of social formations as Baudrillard, among others, convincingly argues.

Jameson's theory of reading as allegorical rewriting says little about distortions and misreadings resulting from either "personal" responses or figural aberrations. He admits to an inadequate account of subjectivity, which partially explains the omission of response theory. About figurative dimensions of discourse, he declares cryptically that "any doctrine of figurality must necessarily be ambiguous: a symbolic expression of a truth is also, at the same time, a distorted and disguised expression, and a theory of figural expression is also a theory of mystification and false consciousness" (70). Although he credits the "distortions" of subjectivity and of figurality, Jameson does not take them into serious account in his theory of reading. Reading is not misreading; it "is here construed as an essentially allegorical act, which consists in rewriting a given text in terms of a particular interpretive master code" (10). For Jameson reading at the level of grammar and rhetoric appears relatively unproblematical. Significantly, he observes, "I have found it possible without any great inconsistency to respect both the methodological imperative implicit in the concept of totality or totalization, and the quite different attention of a 'symptomal' analysis to discontinuities, rifts, actions at a distance, within a merely apparently unified cultural text" (56–57). Texts are heterogeneous, contradictory, and disunified for Jameson primarily on account of contending ideological forces and, as such, they are capable of hermeneutic reunification/totalization, using the three semantic horizons as allegorical transcoding devices. About his special use of the poststructuralist theory of text, Jameson offers a revealing statement which constitutes a veiled response to de Man:

> The type of interpretation here proposed is more satisfactorily grasped as the rewriting of the literary text in such a way that the latter may itself be seen as the rewriting or restructuration of a prior historical or ideological *subtext,* it being always understood that "subtext" is not immediately present as such, not some common-sense external reality. . . . The literary or aesthetic act therefore

always entertains some active relationship with the Real; yet in order to do so, it cannot simply allow "reality" to persevere inertly in its own being, outside the text and at a distance. It must rather draw the Real into its own texture, and the ultimate paradoxes and false problems of linguistics, and most notably of semantics, are to be traced back to this process, whereby language manages to carry the Real within itself as its own intrinsic or immanent subtext. (81)

Since reality comes to us textualized, and since literature retextualizes the subtext of reality, there is no question of the death of the referent. Textualization enacts ideological configurations. Thus figural mystifications conceal/reveal sociopolitical contradictions symptomatic of conflicting classes and modes of production. The task of ideology critique is precisely to "read" out such conflicts. It is noteworthy that this reading has little to do not only with readers' psychology and figural aporias, but also with the history of reception and the role of institutions. All these exclusions limit the impressive scope of Jameson's scheme for cultural analysis.

Critical Reading Close Reading

It seems ironic that certain leading minority theorists of reading complain about the politicization of reading undertaken on behalf of minority literatures whose linguistic complexity and aesthetic richness are purportedly ignored. Let me cite several examples. Gates often self-consciously demonstrates the figural density of African-American texts in an effort to move black criticism away from separatist political polemics and toward exacting close reading in an appreciative mode. "Because of this curious valorization of the social and polemical functions of black literature, the structure of the black text has been *repressed* and treated as if it were *transparent* . . . as if it were invisible, or literal, or a one-dimensional document" (5–6). The insistent figurality of black literature renders reading an arduous task—one best undertaken by literary critics, not sociologists, anthropologists, or folklorists, who skirt poetics in the pursuit of data collection and scientific documentation of "tribal" manners and customs, social structures and political practices. If the failure to "read" black women's texts persists, according to Christian, "our writers will be reduced to illustrations of societal questions or dilemmas, in which people, for the moment, are interested, and will not be valued for their craft, their vision, their work as writers" (149). This neoformalist emphasis on literariness, figurality, and rigorous aesthetic reading aims to counter the tendency to reduce the literatures of blacks, women, and colonized peoples to anthropological or political documents rather than works of art. With Gates, Christian, and others, it is not a question of stressing either sociohistorical significance or aesthetic craft, but both. It is also, more pointedly, a matter of acknowledging the continuing force of long-standing institutionalized norms of *literary* value and of close reading.

To read "closely" in line with the current academic reading formation requires considerable education. To read one must learn to bracket "personal" associations and other such "distortions," to explicate/exploit textual ungrammaticalities, contradictions, and discontinuities, and to construct lucid accounts that orchestrate plot elements, character traits, details of setting, thematic materials, etc. What contemporary academic reading practice needs to do, however, is empower readers to criticize the values and ideologies promoted by texts, question the selections of texts and the processes of selection, explore certain "distortions" and "aberrations" as necessary and valuable materials, study the complex and different temporalities implicated in reading, and scrutinize the many reading protocols widely in use. As it stands, normative academic reading is today often narrowly focused, unduly submissive, overly dutiful, obsessively impersonal, and too accepting of the institutional and social status quo. In my view, an era of *critical* reading has yet to flourish.

7

Figuring (in) Institutions

A significant number of critical theorists have come by various routes in recent years to focus intellectual inquiry on the roles of institutions in the constitution, maintenance, and reproduction of modes of academic study as well as forms of cultural creation. Let me cite several examples. Reader-response critics like Bleich and Fish find that prevailing "styles" of reading are significantly shaped by institutional conventions and practices, leading them to shift scholarly attention from texts to institutions. A similar trajectory is discernible among structuralists like Todorov and Culler, who concentrate not on single works but on the "institution" of literature, specifically on systems of genres and reading protocols. Minority critics, for instance Henderson, JanMohamed, and Gilbert and Gubar, encourage expanding canons, which entails investigations of institutional processes of social exclusion and canon formation. Certain French poststructuralists, particularly Deleuze, Lyotard, and Foucault, expose to view the roles of key social institutions in establishing and maintaining the authoritarian status quo of advanced consumer societies. Numerous leftist critics, Marxist and otherwise, fix attention in their work of ideology critique on constellations of institutions that purvey hegemonic class values and interests. Institutional analysis increasingly characterizes numerous strands of contemporary critical inquiry, and cultural criticism shares in this broad shift of focus away from autonomous texts to the relations of discourses and institutions.

Many of the recurring concepts employed in this book bring to attention, sometimes overtly and sometimes tacitly, institutional dimensions or foundations of cultural phenomena and practices. Among the most obvious of these notions are heteroglossia, social text, regimes of reason, author function, subject-position, generic codes, literature function, and reading conventions. To generalize my view, there is no way to purge from language, literature, and literary study entanglements with numerous institutions. Being situated sociohistorically amidst regimes of reason, authors, readers, and texts are involved more or less with such institutions as schools, families, law courts, churches, publishing firms, book vendors, libraries, theaters, market places, patronage agencies, state offices, media outlets, and censorship bureaus. Insofar as poststructuralist cultural criticism is an academic project, the institution of the university and its neighboring institutions and subinstitutions merit special attention. In fact, the discussions in this book have never strayed for long from institutional matters.

In this chapter I want initially to outline a theory of institutions; thereafter, I shall scrutinize several influential institutional studies, namely two on knowledge/power by Foucault and Said and two on university English studies by Ohmann and Scholes. My aim is to open to view the wide scope and ambitious reach as well as the many complications and problems of institutional analysis and theory. While my position is that cultural criticism must engage in institutional inquiry, the shift to institutional studies among leading contemporary intellectuals neither avoids nor simplifies the difficulties of reading and understanding cultural works. It does, I believe, considerably strengthen criticism if only because it focuses intensely on intricate networks of power and knowledge.

Theory of Institutions

Through various discursive and technical means, institutions constitute and disseminate systems of rules, conventions, and practices that condition the creation, circulation, and use of resources, information, knowledge, and belief. Institutions include, therefore, both material forms and mechanisms of production, distribution, and consumption and ideological norms and protocols shaping the reception, comprehension, and application of discourse. On the material level of the institution of, for example, university literary studies, one would situate such apparatuses as academic publishing companies, bookstores, and libraries, while on the ideological level one would add canonical literary history, classroom pedagogy, and normative critical practice. The point is the discourse of an institution is co-determined by various material and ideological forces and factors: discourse undergoes both commodification and conventionalization; and it, in turn, facilitates both operations. The linkages between such processes of institutionalization, though close, do not always appear to be direct. Institutions, nevertheless, condition the conception, regularization, and employment of knowledge, empowering and authorizing thinking, speaking, writing, reading, and acting by means of codified "dos" and "don'ts" as well as rewards and punishments. Institutions participate in and preside over the production and allocation of knowledge and power within and across regimes of reason.

Specific institutions characteristically have relations with other institutions, sharing networks of continuities and discontinuities that enable and inhibit various functions. In any given situation, such sets of institutions may exhibit different genealogies, each displaying individual stages of formation and development. In addition, any one institution may itself consist of various subinstitutions and partial institutions in the same way that its hierarchy of guiding concepts may vary from one moment to another and one location to another. The addition of the complex of other historical (sometimes transnational) institutions to the specific institution makes plain the characteristically complicated dynamics faced by analysts of institutions.

Institutions often enable things to function, inaugurate new modes of knowledge, initiate productive associations, offer assistance and support, provide useful information, create helpful social ties, simplify large-scale problems, protect the vulnerable, and enrich the community. Social life in the absence of institutions is unthinkable. Without institutions there is no community. Typically, institutions explain events, normalize behavior, regulate values, promote efficiency, package information, organize interests, centralize authority, hier-archize constituents, erect borders, prescribe pleasure, license play, institute discipline, banish deviance, maintain the status quo, engage in self-promotion, rationalize particular interests, bureaucratize thought and activity, solicit obedience, mechanize bodies, engender opposition. The dynamics of institutions frequently tend toward abuse.

The abusive practices of tightly overlapping institutions, apparent at all levels of contemporary Western societies, create among a grow-ing number of intellectuals an anti-institutional ethicopolitics critical of reigning regimes of reason, which reproduce the oppressive institu-tional status quo so insistently that an anarchistic or libertarian poli-tics, or something like it, appears increasingly common among the expanding ranks of oppositional critics. The various turns to cultural criticism, and particularly to cultural critique, which characterize much criticism in recent decades, widely exhibit an ethos of suspicion regarding institutions often indebted for its theoretical articulation to Foucault. I count myself among such critics.

Apparatuses of Knowledge/Power

I want to focus my discussion of Foucault primarily on the final pages of *Discipline and Punish,* which describe the paradigmatic "carceral system" that developed along with the formation of the penitentiary between 1760 and 1840. The legacy of the Enlightenment and still with us after two centuries, the carceral combines into a continuum and archipelago numerous institutions, including the military, judi-cial, educational, psychiatric, welfare, and prison establishments, all of which enforce norms and correct delinquencies using similar tech-niques and rationalities.

> Prison continues, on those who are entrusted to it, a work begun elsewhere, which the whole of society pursues on each individual through innumerable mechanisms of discipline. By means of a car-ceral continuum, the authority that sentences infiltrates all those other authorities that supervise, transform, correct, improve. (302–3)

It is this complex ensemble that constitutes the "carceral system," not only the institution of the prison, with its walls, its staff, its regulations and its violence. The carceral system combines in a single figure discourses and architecture, coercive regulations and scientific propositions, real social effects and invincible utopias, programmes for correcting delinquents and mechanisms that reinforce delinquency. (271)

We have seen that, in penal justice, the prison transformed the punitive procedure into a penitentiary technique; the carceral archipelago transported this technique from the penal institution to the entire social body. (298)

The judges of normality are present everywhere. We are in the society of the teacher-judge, the doctor-judge, the educator-judge, the "social worker"-judge; it is on them that the universal reign of the normative is based; and each individual, wherever he may find himself, subjects to it his body, his gestures, his behaviour, his aptitudes, his achievements. The carceral network, in its compact or disseminated forms, with its systems of insertion, distribution, surveillance, observation, has been the greatest support, in modern society, of the normalizing power. (304)

The dispositions of disciplined bodies in military ranks, prison cells, orphanages, hospital wards, church assemblies, and classroom rows exhibit a certain uniform order in which subjects are made available to observation, improvement, correction, normalization. While sanctions exist to manage deviances and insure docility, the carceral characteristically coerces with kindness and delicacy, employing finely graduated mechanisms of punishment and rarely relying on torture or severe bodily punishment.

The portrait of the carceral, persuasive and unforgettable, is yet monolithic. Foucault's project has problems, though I shall delineate neither the numerous attacks upon it, nor Foucault's various responses. It leaves little room for resistance or transformation, not to mention revolution. Implicitly, it counsels quietism, as many of Foucault's critics note. The claim that each individual subjects herself or himself to the "universal reign of the normative" is a characteristic

exaggeration. Moreover, the notions that all aberrations and delinquencies occur within the system and that they are calculated to do so
similarly accord little possibility for opposition and change. With
Foucault the era of oppositional politics appears at an end; the sub-
dued masses can be counted out. Another problem with Foucault's
presentation is that it seems to discount the effectivity of local subver-
sions, manipulations, and creative misuses of the system. Not surprisingly, activists find Foucault overly despondent. Finally, Foucault's
account of institutional *discourse* is at once useful and limited. Its
usefulness comes both in its delineations of the constituting and excluding forces of language and in its depictions of the inauguration of
knowledge and power effected through disciplinary discourses. In its
instrumentalist views, however, this theory of discourse minimizes
such disruptive phenomena as rhetoricity, heteroglossia, misreading,
and distortion. Ironically, Foucault capitulates to the technocratic
normalization of discourse by downplaying its "delinquencies."

Foucault's dramatic rendition of the knowledge/power nexus continues to galvanize theorists of institutions. It will be recalled
Foucault urges us to understand "that power and knowledge directly
imply one another; that there is no power relation without the correla-
tive constitution of a field of knowledge, nor any knowledge that does
not presuppose and constitute at the same time power relations" (27).
What characterizes knowledge/power is not simply the traditional
negativities of repression, exclusion, and abstraction. Positively,
knowledge/power produces reality, constituting fields of objects and
protocols of rationality. One can witness such a concatenation operating in the widespread use since the Enlightenment era of "tables," to
name just one of many modalities of knowledge/power singled out by
Foucault. Tables are employed to construct taxonomies of biological
entities, to observe and control the flows of commodities and curren-
cies, to make classifications of diseases and allocate hospital spaces.
The table is "both a technique of power and a procedure of knowledge" (148). Developed and extended by the carceral, this technology
of power provides a means of analyzing and mastering multiplicities.

With Foucault knowledge loses its traditional honorific status, becoming a suspect counterpart of power and authority.

To explore the impact of Foucault's theorizing on knowledge/ power and to consider a widely emulated model of institutional analysis, I shall turn to Said's *Orientalism*. "For students of literature and criticism," declares Said, "Orientalism offers a marvelous instance of the interrelations between society, history, and textuality; moreover, the cultural role played by the Orient in the West connects Orientalism with ideology, politics, and the logic of power, matters of relevance, I think, to the literary community" (24). Said illustrates how scholarly knowledge works in the interest of coercive power: the discipline of Orientalism serves the post-Enlightenment colonization by Western countries of large sections of the Eastern world. Scholarship and discourse emerge as instruments of conquest.

> Taking the late eighteenth century as a very roughly defined starting point Orientalism can be discussed and analyzed as the corporate institution for dealing with the Orient—dealing with it by making statements about it, authorizing views of it, describing it, by teaching it, settling it, ruling over it: in short, Orientalism as a Western style for dominating, restructuring, and having authority over the Orient. . . . My contention is that without examining Orientalism as a discourse one cannot possibly understand the enormously systematic discipline by which European culture was able to manage—and even produce—the Orient politically, sociologically, militarily, ideologically, scientifically, and imaginatively. . . . Moreover, so authoritative a position did Orientalism have that I believe no one writing, thinking, or acting on the Orient could do so without taking account of the limitations on thought and action imposed by Orientalism. (3)

Orientalism is an institution, meaning a systematic historical discourse constituting and controlling its "object" through administrative agencies that collect and allocate knowledge and power. This "institution" consists not only of universities, government services, trading companies, geographical societies, missionary teams, and research foundations but also of regulatory codes, classifications, refer-

ence sources, journals, translations, travelogues, and accredited representations. In its recent postwar American version, the carceral-like
institution of Orientalism lives on, according to Said, in the form of
the "Middle East studies establishment, a pool of interests, 'old boy'
or 'expert' networks linking corporate business, the foundations, the
oil companies, the missions, the military, the foreign service, the intelligence community together with the academic world. There are
grants and other rewards, there are organizations, there are hierarchies, there are institutes, centers, faculties, departments, all devoted to legitimizing and maintaining the authority of a handful of
basic, basically unchanging ideas about Islam, the Orient, and the
Arabs" (301–2).

As a consequence of Orientalism, the subject-positions of both colonial others from the "Orient" and Western people become rigidified
and generic. Stereotypes reign. The Oriental person is first an Oriental and second a human being. An analogous generic identification
pertains to the Westerner. A Manichean dynamic rules relations. A
Palestinian living in the diaspora, Said experiences Orientalism as "all
aggression, activity, judgment, will-to-truth, and knowledge" (204).
In thrall to Orientalist understanding, Westerners exhibit racism,
ethnocentrism, and imperialism. By distinguishing between latent
and manifest Orientalism, Said accounts for the steadfastness of Western stereotyping: "Whatever change occurs in knowledge of the Orient is found almost exclusively in manifest Orientalism; the unanimi-
ty, stability, and durability of latent Orientalism are more or less
constant" (206). Significantly, latent Orientalism affects most
present-day Orientalist scholars whose work is constrained by the institution and whose statements are regulated: "One does not really
make discourse at will, or statements in it, without first belonging—
in some cases unconsciously, but at any rate involuntarily—to the
ideology and institutions that guarantee its existence" (321).

Whereas Said's general characterization and genealogy of the institution of Orientalism are persuasive, his explicit criticism is troubling because it contradicts his best insights. In criticizing Orientalism, he often backtracks from Foucauldian poststructuralist positions

to humanistic existential and empirical stances where he has recourse
to the dubious concept of "authentic experience." From this perspective the purported trouble with Orientalism is that it does not attend
to so-called observable reality. Here are seven among other such examples.

> There were—and are—cultures and nations whose location is in
> the East, and their lives, histories, and customs have a brute reality
> obviously greater than anything that could be said about them in
> the West. (5)

> It seems a common human failing to prefer the schematic authority
> of a text to the disorientations of direct encounters with the human.
> (93)

> The contemporary intellectual can learn from Orientalism how, on
> the one hand, either to limit or to enlarge realistically the scope of
> his discipline's claims, and on the other, to see the human ground
> (the foul-rag-and-bone shop of the heart, Yeats called it) in which
> texts, visions, methods, and disciplines begin, grow, thrive, and
> degenerate. (110)

> Orientalists are neither interested in nor capable of discussing indi-
> viduals. . . . Marx is no exception. The collective Orient was
> easier for him to use in illustration of a theory than existential hu-
> man identities. (154–55)

> What these widely diffused notions of the Orient depended on was
> the almost total absence in contemporary Western culture of the
> Orient as a genuinely felt and experienced force. (208)

> Since an Arab poet or novelist—and there are many—writes of his
> experiences, of his values, of his humanity (however strange that
> may be), he effectively disrupts the various patterns (images,
> clichés, abstractions) by which the Orient is represented. A literary
> text speaks more or less directly of living reality. (291)

> The study of man in society is based on concrete human history and
> experience, not on donnish abstractions, or on obscure laws or arbi-
> trary systems. The problem then is to make the study fit and in
> some way be shaped by the experience. (327–28)

The traditional humanistic manner of thinking here depends on the classical logocentric binary "reality/language" where language reflects or distorts preexisting concrete, brute, direct, personal, individual, living reality. Poets successfully talk of reality while intellectuals typically pen distortions, clichés, stereotypes, arbitrary schemes, and abstract laws. (Bardolatry lives on with Said.) To cure such ills, intellectuals must 1) focus on individuals rather than collectivities, 2) practice scrupulous perception of the real to which scholarly words must correspond, 3) avoid images, representations, systems, disciplines, 4) engage in purifying self-reflection and methodological skepticism, and 5) adopt individualistic oppositional stances "beyond" disciplines. To reiterate, this humanistic credo of discredited notions empowers Said's explicit criticisms of Orientalism; the poststructuralist ideas prompting his critical genealogy of the institution of Orientalism are, however, remarkably different: 1) study collectivities, 2) uncover systems of representation in cultural archives, 3) attend to conventions, codes, and practices of disciplines, 4) acknowledge (being imbricated in regimes of reason) the limits of self-reflection and the durabilities of social constructions, and 5) mount critiques from the vantage of "a libertarian, or a nonrepressive and nonmanipulative, perspective" (24), specifically that of an Oriental subject, an exiled spokesperson for the Palestinian people.

It is quite common among certain ethnic critics, feminist scholars, and postcolonial theorists, as earlier chapters note, to contrast existential realities with pernicious cultural stereotypes as a means of grounding critique. This is an important and valuable tactic in the struggle over cultural representations. But "existential reality," in poststructuralist terms, amounts to a particularly questionable sociohistorical discursive construction of subjectivity/collectivity. There is no getting around representation. In his better moments, Said appreciates this point:

> The real issue is whether indeed there can be a true representation
> of anything, or whether any and all representations, because they
> *are* representations, are embedded first in the language and then in
> the culture, institutions, and political ambience of the repre-

senter. . . . What this must lead us to methodologically is to
view representations (or misrepresentations—the distinction is at
best a matter of degree) as inhabiting a common field of play defined for them, not by some inherent common subject matter
alone, but by some common history, tradition, universe of discourse. (272–73)

Discursive communities construct cultural (mis)representations. "Reality" is itself such a construct. Prediscursive reality is a fictitious
back-formation, an old dream neatly partitioning nature/culture.
The institutions of communal languages give us realities. Despite
Said's regressive wishes, "presentation" is always representation, a
neighbor of misrepresentation. Language does not ruin "presentation" by making it representation/misrepresentation. Written language is not original sin nor is oral presentation Edenic truth. Unlike
Foucault, Said intermittently believes so.

The Institution of English Studies

For cultural critics the institutional analysis of academic literary studies continues to be indebted to Ohmann's pioneering *English in America* and Scholes's *Textual Power*. Like Said's scrutiny of Orientalism,
Ohmann's investigation of English studies presents a grim assessment
of the growing professionalization of knowledge and careerism among
intellectuals. Both critics find the university in complicity with other
institutions like the military, judicial system, intelligence community, industrial economy, and government bureaucracy in maintaining an authoritarian, racist, and imperialistic status quo. Both
also single out for criticism the subordinate service functions per-
formed by granting agencies, presses, disciplinary journals, professional organizations, pedagogical anthologies, "think tanks," and factitious departmentalizations. In Althusser's terms, Said and Ohmann
portray contemporary higher education as, in large part, an ideological state apparatus.

Ohmann is explicit about his enterprise. "The point is to understand some of the *institutions* that are most responsible for the trans-

mission of literacy and culture. Their forms often reveal more about culture than do public pronouncements on the humanities, art and society, audiences and interpretation" (3–4). Furthermore, "institutions don't exist in vacuums or in the pure atmosphere of their ideals. They are part of the social order and survive by helping to maintain it" (22). The functions served by contemporary university English departments meet the needs of the industrial state, the technostructure, and related organizations. For instance, departments help eliminate "the less adapted, the ill-trained, the city youth with bad verbal manners, blacks with the wrong dialect, Latinos with the wrong language, and the rebellious in all shapes and sizes, thus helping to maintain social and economic inequalities" (230). Moreover, departments teach elites attitudes of caution, cooperation, and detachment and skills of organization, analysis, and practical writing. Elites are prepared to serve with civility. With regard to reading literature, the model student "focuses on a character, on the poet's attitude, on the individual's struggle toward understanding—but rarely, if ever, on the social forces that are revealed in every dramatic scene and almost every stretch of narration in fiction. Power, class, culture, social order and disorder—these staples of all literature are quite excluded from consideration" (59–60). The restricted modes of literacy purveyed by universities reenforce the current deployment of knowledge/power in the interests of control, domination, and profit-taking: "A society generates such knowledge mainly when there is economic demand for it. And economic demand, in our system, is expressed through the drive for profit and autonomy of those individuals and corporations who control the manufacture of goods. We get the knowledge they need, as well as that the government needs to protect the stability of the system itself. . . . But there is no paradox in adding that this same knowledge blocks liberation and diminishes power for most human beings" (323).

Ohmann self-consciously writes from the position of a white middle-class professor, who from within the elite university system seeks change. Reluctantly, says Ohmann, he has come to see the need for social revolution. "We either teach politically with revolution as our end or we contribute to the mystification that so often in universities diverts and deadens the critical power of literature and encysts it in our safe corner of society" (335). Short of revolution, there are things to be done. For example, Ohmann urges us "not to destroy professional ramparts, but to reach out over them—selectively—to poor people, minority races, workers, and in so doing build alliances that may save and humanize the intellectual life in bad times shortly to come" (252*n*). Also we can seek "to educate students as critics of our verbal culture; to give them an understanding of the fictions . . . we tell one another, which give direction to our politics, our work, and all our acts; to nourish self-understanding and self-realization as literature supposedly can do" (224). But like Foucault and Said, Ohmann is basically pessimistic about the prospects of reform, a mood recurrent among institutional analysts, who in bad moments risk paranoia, seeing institutional conspiracies in constant formation.

In the opening chapter of *Textual Power,* Scholes sketches a suggestive institutional model of the English department, a model inspired largely by Foucault's work. No mention is made of Ohmann, and Said's work on Orientalism is overlooked. Using the resources of structuralist theory, Scholes writes:

> I propose that we consider "English" as a generic concept, an epistemic institution or apparatus that limits and enables the specific manifestations of "English" as a discipline or field of study, including its political embodiment in this or that English department, each of which can be seen as a political and economic instance of a generic arche-department. (3)

> The arche-institution of English lives in each one of us as a professional unconscious. (4)

What most characterizes the academic institution of English studies are two sets of hierarchical oppositions—"literature/non-literature" and "consumption/production." As Scholes reminds us, the interpretation of literary texts is systematically privileged over the writing of compositions (consumption/literature versus production/non-literature). This system of valorization manifests itself in pay scales, work loads, curricula design, and certain discriminatory practices. Women are clustered in the ranks of lower-paid faculty teaching numerous sections of composition. Better-paid men dominate the ranks of those teaching fewer classes of literary interpretations. Specialists in popular works (pseudo-literature) and film (non-literature), like those in professional and technical writing, generally occupy nonprestigious positions. The institution of "English" values and authorizes studying particular objects and activities while tolerating or devaluing certain others. The ideology of the institution reveals itself also in such mundane matters as differential allocations of office space, travel support, research funds, titles, awards, and honors.

Having learned from Frye, Derrida, and Jameson, as well as Foucault, Scholes refers to the paradigm of the English department as, alternately, a genre, arche-form, system, apparatus, institution, and discipline—lodged in the professional unconscious. Although he decides against tracing the genealogy of the institution (on this enterprise see Graff), he occasionally links its broader formation and functioning with religion, economics, sociology, politics, history, epistemology, ethics, and, of course, education.

Scholes is preoccupied with future reforms of the English department, not its past history. He rules out revolution: "I find myself looking for a middle ground between reform and revolution. The most radical talk often produces the least action or generates an overwhelming reaction, thus becoming literally counterproductive" (10). The strategy is to rebuild the apparatus; the tactics include maintaining civility while revising traditional ideas and values. The primary goal is to turn out students able to mount not only competent readings and interpretations but effective cultural critiques of many modes of discourse, ranging from canonical novels to classic films and from magazine ads to television programs: "The exclusivity of literature as a category must be discarded. All kinds of texts, visual as well as verbal, polemical as well as seductive, must be taken as the occasion for further textuality. And textual studies must be pushed beyond the discrete boundaries of the page and the book into the institutional practices and social structures" (16–17). Scholes associates this enterprise with the secular worldly criticism of contemporary leftists. In his view, "interpretation involves connecting the singular oppositions of the text to the generalized oppositions that structure our cultural systems of values. In other words, we are talking about ideology" (33). Properly conceived, textual criticism requires irreverent and skeptical critiques of institutions and ideologies. This project of transformation depends on the linkage of text with social text and on the understanding of critical reading as intellectual production, both of which break down the literature/non-literature and the consumption/production oppositions.

Like other contemporary cultural critics and theorists of academic institutions, Scholes seeks not simply to expand the primary "object" of analysis from literature to textuality, but to transform the "object" from aesthetic artifact to cultural discourse. And he aims to supplement normative explicative and exegetical methods of analysis with institutional and ideological analysis. This whole enterprise is constructed explicitly against the neutral historical scholarship and formalist criticism dominant in the postwar university. Most of the inspiration and many of the critical instruments to effect this change derive from structuralist and poststructuralist theories. However, Scholes draws on a remarkably limited range of this thinking and finds much to criticize in it.

In the area of language theory, to take one key topic, Bakhtin is not mentioned, Barthes is minimized, and de Man and Jameson are roundly attacked. There are serious limitations with Scholes's project. To start with, Scholes's theorizing about language offers a faint sense of discourse as a heteroglot site of cultural differentiation and struggle. In addition, the intertext is effectively limited to known cultural codes and interpretive traditions—the heterogeneity, contradictoriness, and infinity of intertextuality never emerge as serious possibilities. The vexing rhetoricity of texts is denied in a misreading of de Man who is erroneously said to "see texts as radically self-reflective and non-referential" (76) and to grant "the special status of literature only to texts that are innocent of contamination by reference to the world" (77). Scholes's own quite traditional position is that the world is knowable, that texts are intelligible, and that we regularly make contact with empirical objects and with realities. For him there exists an "untextualized world" (62). Accordingly, Jameson's idea that "history" is inaccessible to us except in textual form is condemned because it is "reluctant to emerge from its own web of textuality to make contact with the world" (84). By restraining heteroglossia, intertextuality, rhetoricity, and textuality, Scholes tames the poststructuralist project, instrumentalizing language, simplifying discourse and its entanglements with regimes of reason, dismissing the phenomenon of misreading, and ultimately recasting criticism as a born-again ethical humanism.

Scholes sometimes problematically invokes the generic "human." Let us examine two instances. Faced with the question of whether or not to teach Hemingway, Scholes decides in the affirmative, provided his work is "properly balanced by other writers, for instance writers whose texts will be more appealing to female students" (58) and provided teachers realize "it is Hemingway's fallibility that makes him so useful in the curriculum. Or rather, it is his combination of strength and weakness, his considerable rhetorical skill and formal control combined with a very disputable set of values: it is his humanity, if you will, that makes him interesting" (59). What constitutes "humanity"? Evidently, aesthetic prowess mixed with dubious ideology. General fallibility. Scholes tells us in another more revealing instance: "Human beings become human through the acquisition of language, and this acquisition alienates humans from all those things that language names. The name is a substitute for the thing; it displaces the thing in the very act of naming it, so that language finally stands even between one human being and another. Much of our poetry has been written to undo this condition, to remove the veil of language that covers everything" (112). Surprisingly, humanity is portrayed as a state of alienation from things and others through language, as a state that poetry seeks to correct by lifting the linguistic shroud that drapes over things and others. This is a replay of a sad and nostalgic Enlightenment aesthetic rooted in Christian humanism. Prior to language was this utopian state of prelapsarian communion with nature and the brotherhood of man. Language ruined all that. This fable gives us original sin without the burden of orthodox Christian dogma. Once man was glorious and strong but now he is ignoble and weak—that is "humanity," which is what aesthetics and poetics are all about. Miraculously, much poetry attempts to show us the evils of linguistic alienation through language. Fallibility is what we teach. Such strands of conservative thinking occasionally crop up in "poststructuralist" theorizing, as noted in chapter 1 when discussing Miller.

In Kristeva's contending Lacanian account, the advent of language, it will be recalled, signals the emergence of the unconscious, the differentiation of the body, and the entry into symbolic realms, all of which open the subject to heteroglot sociopolitical spheres complete with institutions, including the institutions of patriarchy, property ownership, law, family, religion, and so on. To be named is to be officially enrolled in regimes of reason characterized by overlapping, often porous, institutions and ideologies. Here is a fable more suited to Scholes's best insights. The old story of man's fall into language as an alienation from community and from authentic existence is badly flawed. It gives us, once again, the cursed and isolated individual of religious humanism.

Textual Power is a pedagogical guide designed to persuade professors teaching undergraduate English to practice cultural criticism. It illustrates how to move from explication and exegesis to cultural critique. It frankly characterizes this as a move to ideological analysis, justifying it in the name of proper ethics and citizenship education. *Textual Power* is both a helpful and an influential book, which I regularly recommend to colleagues and which I take seriously enough to criticize as a primer for cultural criticism. It does offer a suggestive model of the "English apparatus," enabling a critique of the institution of English studies. What is missing from this model is a critique of professionalism of the sort initiated by Ohmann. More importantly, the conceptualization of institutions seems timid and impoverished. An antithetical understanding appears in Foucault's delineation of the "carceral archipelago," where large numbers of institutions overlap and cooperate in a far-reaching nexus of knowledge and power. The vast productive and repressive forces of institutional networks, variously illustrated by Foucault, Ohmann, and Said, simply do not appear with Scholes. The English apparatus is isolated, dehistoricized, and depoliticized. Nothing critical is said about the university, the government, the economy, the military, the foundations, the publishers, etc. Like other institutional analysts, Scholes displays no interest in exceptional or marginal cases: among the roughly three thousand English departments in America, for example, certain aberrations surely deserve attention for what they reveal about the crevices and "weak spots" in the institution. What is minor goes unattended. In the absence of a sense of regimes of reason or something similar, Scholes's recommendation for institutional analysis as an essential aspect of cultural criticism disappointingly fails to show the way and, in fact, presents a misleading example. An extensive network and concatenation of institutions enable and constrain the English apparatus. Critique should neither stop nor seem to stop at the fragile and shifting "internal" borders of the discipline; when it does so, as it does here, it enacts a repetition of "intrinsic criticism" at the level of institutions.

Institutional Analysis and Cultural Critique

In casting about for promising theories of institutional analysis (poststructuralist and otherwise), I encountered much disheartening material, illustrating many problems that arise with even the most thoughtful work on institutions. As an instance, I shall very briefly single out difficulties posed by the work of Grant Webster, drawing concluding lessons from this example.

Advocating a new mode of institutional analysis to write the history of modern critical schools, Webster constructs a model consisting of five stages of historical development in the formation of schools (ideological period, critical revolution, normal criticism, crisis in criticism, and obsolescence). Each stage has significant substages, which I shall not detail. Mapped onto the disciplinary model is another model of four stages in an exemplary professional career (apprenticeship, journeyman, man of letters, and superannuation). Using these models, Webster finds many interesting things to say about the roles of journals, the dynamics of canon formation, the rituals of professionalism, and the relativity of critical paradigms. However, the connections between critical schools and society are largely skirted. Given his models, much of his pragmatic work is ultimately devoted to reputation studies and professional biography, tracing the rises and falls of illustrious members of select critical communities. At one point Webster muses on the consequences of critics accepting the inevitable obsolescence of their work:

> The first consequence would surely be a lowering of the ideological temperature, so that critics would no longer conceive of their remarks in an implicitly metaphysical or theological context, which sees literary criticism leading to Truth or Salvation. Critics would then perhaps cultivate the virtue of humility. Second, the relative relationship between criticism and literature would be changed; criticism would again become a dependent art, and would be justified as it contributed to the illumination of literary works or literary culture . . . the ultimate standard would become practical application in reinterpreting the literary tradition rather than theoretical interest and complexity. (59)

Here institutional analysis retains key values of orthodox academic study. What remains important are civility, humility, duty, practicality, tradition. Avoiding theoretical complexity, I shall draw a lesson from this example: institutional analysis in the absence of cultural critique risks recapitulating the reigning value system of normal criticism. Nothing much gets disturbed. We are back at humble exegesis of masterpieces. A positive supplement must be attached to the lesson: institutional analysis informed by poststructuralist cultural critique, whatever its specific orientations and particular problems, constitutes a potential advance by virtue of its work of questioning institutional hierarchies, interests, exclusions, procedures, and norms.

I want to close this line of thinking with several other supplements. Another name for différance is *instituting*. "There is nothing outside of the text" means there is no escaping institutions. We are only just beginning to figure in institutions.

8

Reconnoitering Birmingham Cultural Studies

The numerous and diverse works produced by members and associates of the influential Centre for Contemporary Cultural Studies (CCCS) at the University of Birmingham constitute an important archive of pioneering materials for intellectuals seeking to promote the practice of cultural criticism as well as the new discipline of cultural studies. Several directors of the Centre, namely Hall in the 1970s and Johnson in the 1980s, agree in separate synoptic articles that two modes of cultural inquiry characterize the research undertaken at the Centre from the sixties to the eighties, the golden years. The "culturalist" mode, derived from sociology, anthropology, and social history, and influenced by the homegrown work of Hoggart, Thompson, and Williams, regards a culture as a whole way of life and struggle accessible through detailed concrete (empirical) descriptions that capture the unities of commonplace cultural forms and material experience. The "structuralist" mode, indebted to French linguistics, literary criticism, and semiotic theory, and especially attentive to texts by Althusser, Barthes, and Foucault, conceives of cultural forms as (semi)autonomous inaugurating "discourses" susceptible to rhetorical and semiological analyses of cognitive constitutions and ideological effects. What distinguishes CCCS research in latter years is an attempt to employ both modes of inquiry, using Gramscian theory as a bridge. To get at some key contributions and limitations of this multifaceted model project, I want to focus primarily on Hebdige's major book, *Hiding in the Light: On Images and Things,* an exemplary collection of related articles from the eighties that examines paradigmatic cultural discourses and explores pressing theoretical issues. Hebdige is a leading figure of the school in its heyday. Without negating their individuality or originality, Hebdige's researches, sometimes provocative and sometimes vexing, derive from and typify much that is characteristic of CCCS work. The topics to be discussed in this chapter, regularly of concern to Birmingham scholars, include the concepts of cultural circuits, poststructuralism, popular culture, "affective alliances," subculture, and Marxist critique. It will be evident from this case study that, though I am sympathetic with Birmingham cultural studies, I find some serious problems with this landmark development in contemporary cultural criticism.

Protocol of Entanglement

What I call the "protocol of entanglement," fundamental to all kinds of cultural criticisms, is a methodological tactic that construes objects and phenomena always in relation to complex temporal and spatial contiguities and proximities. From the vantage of this critical protocol what is unimaginable is an artifact or event without links to regimes of reason. Absolute autonomy is an aestheticist fiction. Despite the insistence on linkages, however, certain cultural critics decline to level objects and phenomena or to study vernacular or quotidian arts, urging that only the best that has been thought and said deserves attention. For such critics, leveling is a disaster. Birmingham cultural studies not only links but levels and herein lies a distinctive feature of its enterprise.

The objects of study typical of Birmingham cultural studies include such popular, low, and mass cultural forms as advertisements, everyday architectural spaces, cartoons, conversations, product designs, fashions, youth subcultures, popular literary genres (romances, thrillers, science fiction), magazines, movies, rock musics, performance arts, photos, postcards, radio, television, and video. Such "humble" topics bear witness to the legacy of Marxist sociological studies informing CCCS inquiry. Programmatically, the arts of the street and the marketplace displace those of the traditional museum and library. Among the predominant modes of inquiry are ethnographic descriptions, "textual" explications, field interviews, group surveys, and ideological and institutional analyses. In carrying out inquiries, such key concepts as commodification, cooption, hegemony, and resistance function as main speculative instruments. Set against the purifying aestheticist drive to isolate and monumentalize art objects is the counter impulse to level and link cultural objects into complex material networks. The notion of *cultural circuits,* self-consciously employed by Birmingham scholars, sets the protocol of entanglement to work by promoting scrutiny of interlocking but discrete processes of production, distribution, and consumption. There is nothing outside cultural circuits.

In his celebrated earlier book, *Subculture: The Meaning of Style,* Hebdige illustrates how the spectacular styles of postwar subcultures of English working-class youths, particularly teddy boys, mods, rockers, skinheads, and punks, challenge obliquely social consensus, normalization, ideology, and hegemony, functioning through displacement as symbolic forms of dissent and resistance. This book was influenced by the Centre's earlier collective *Resistance Through Rituals: Youth Subcultures in Post-War Britain* and Willis's *Learning to Labour: How Working Class Kids Get Working Class Jobs.* Style, in Hebdige's suggestive formulation, consists of special disruptive combinations of dress, argot, music, and dance, often "adopted" by white youths from marginal black groups like Rastafarians, and frequently subject to cooption and mainstreaming by being turned into products for mass markets. As a critic working in the CCCS tradition, Hebdige conceives style to be a complex material and aesthetic ensemble linked with specifiable historical and socioeconomic forces, possessing demonstrable semiotic values and ideological valences, all potentially subject to diffusion, routinization, and commodification by means of the agencies and institutions of established society. Here as elsewhere in the Centre's scholarship, the aesthetic and the social, innovation and history, avant-garde and lower class, creative words and common gripes, disco and assembly line nestle together inseparably and inevitably.

The protocol of entanglement conditions not only the objects selected for study, but the parameters set upon cultural inquiry. Commenting on Barthes's investigation in *Mythologies* into a new Citröen automobile, Hebdige concludes that "the 'cultural significance' of the Citröen DS 19 might be defined as the sum total of all the choices and fixings made at each stage in the passage of the object from conception, production and mediation to mass-circulation, sale and use" (82). To get at this significance, according to Hebdige, an analyst must examine such specific items as engineering design, relations of design team to management, market and motivational research, changes in design, limits of technological resources, plant modifications, labor processes, exhibitions and press conferences, handouts and releases, ad campaigns, press reviews, retail arrangements, domestic and foreign distribution, servicing facilities, prices, sales figures, target groups, and competitors. Each moment in this particular circuit is independent yet interlocking. One phase may predominate. Contradictions can emerge. What this example illustrates is that neither the product, nor its consumption, nor its distribution gains the analytical center. In literary critical terms, neither formalism, nor receptionism, nor sociology of art plays a singular role in inquiry; each finds a use in the project of Birmingham cultural studies. For Hebdige the analyst is situated amid (not above) objects and images, things and signs, with the task of investigating/investing particulars and details in relation to structures and molar formations. The practice of scrutinizing targeted artifacts and phenomena in connection with specific arrays of relevant cultural circuits sets up the scope of inquiry in such a way as to foreground the culturally symbolic dimensions of particular items. Nothing stands beyond culture.

Poststructuralism and Popular Culture

It is not surprising that in *Hiding in the Light* Hebdige offers a chapter on British postwar pop art and one on *The Face* (a widely circulated postmodern-style magazine of the eighties), since both instantiate popular entangling genres. As he isolates significant traits, Hebdige maps them onto larger cultural circuits. In the course of isolating and mapping, he reveals a bifurcated response to processes of entanglement. Pop art receives praise; *The Face* gets condemned. In the latter case, certain values become especially clear: Hebdige deplores the solipsism often fostered by consumer culture and its arts. Equating poststructuralism with postmodernism, he criticizes both for a whole spectrum of alleged evils. What emerges from these memorable inquiries is a critical assessment of influential popular arts constructed in harmony with a certain ethicopolitical line of thinking common among CCCS intellectuals. The vehemence of Hebdige's responses, negative and positive, renders him at once eccentric and representative. Let me start with pop art and move on to *The Face* and to poststructuralism. I am interested in tracing a vacillating pattern of critical evaluations regarding popular culture—a pattern that reveals a particular position common among contemporary humanist critics on the left, including those associated with Birmingham.

A reaction against modernism, pop art returns to representational visual communication, celebrating the superficial and accessible rather than the profound and difficult while displaying fascination with mass-produced images and common everyday products. Pop art overturns the traditional hierarchy of the arts by setting decorative art and graphics on a par with so-called fine art, by replacing the tone of high seriousness with an irreverent sense of play, and by blurring the lines between the categories of high and low, aesthetic and nonaesthetic, creative and commercial. In Hebdige's approving words, "pop formed up at the interface between the analysis of 'popular culture' and the production of 'art,' on the turning point between those two opposing definitions of culture: culture as a standard of excellence, culture as a descriptive category" (125).

From the outset the conservative left has condemned pop art, a fact which Hebdige, a Marxist like other Birmingham intellectuals, finds troubling. Among the purported problems with such art are its capitulations to the illusions of affluent bourgeois society, slick advertising and commercialization, the gallery system and the artist as star, frivolous fashion and callow pleasure. This pious dismissal of pop art in Hebdige's insightful assessment "merely reproduces unaltered the ideological distinction between, on the one hand, the 'serious,' the 'artistic,' the 'political,' and, on the other, the 'ephemeral,' the 'commercial,' the 'pleasurable'—a set of distinctions which pop art itself exposed as being, at the very least, open to question, distinctions which pop practice set out to erode" (126). Hebdige locates a large part of the positive iconoclastic power of pop art in its exposure and subversion of the grounds of "good taste," which he like Bourdieu rightly construes as a social, economic, and political formation as much as an aesthetic one. By policing the link between serious and frivolous art, certain left critics end up doing work for various establishments. To deplore popular culture—the consumption of widely disseminated artifacts, films, records, fashions, TV shows, etc.—is to miss its critical force and solidify anew the elitist account of culture against the interests of ordinary people.

Hebdige is not an enthusiastic supporter of all the popular arts produced in the postwar era of consumption. He is on occasion very critical, as in the revealing case of *The Face*.

> *The Face* is a magazine that goes out of its way every month to blur the line between politics and parody and pastiche; the street, the stage, the screen; between purity and danger; the mainstream and the "margins": to flatten out the world.
>
> For flatness is corrosive and infectious. . . . In the land of the gentrified cut-up, as in the place of dreams, anything imaginable can happen, anything at all. The permutations are unlimited: high/low/folk/popular culture; pop music/opera; street fashion/advertising/*haute couture;* journalism/science fiction/critical theory. . . .
>
> With the sudden loss of gravity, the lines that hold these terms apart waver and collapse. Such combinations are as fragile, as impermanent as the categories of which they are composed; the entire structure is a house made of cards. It's difficult to retain a faith in anything much at all when absolutely *everything* moves with the market. (161)

Like pop art, the pop journalism in *The Face* revels in entangling genres employing collage and pastiche, linking widely dispersed heterogeneous domains, and leveling distinctions and hierarchies. It prefers flows to fixities, surfaces to depths, floating to gravity, movement to order. But this liquefaction of "reality" is so extreme, iconoclastic, and infectious as to engender a general collapse. It leaves no footholds to mount critiques. It tacitly counsels resignation, solipsism, fatalism. Significantly, Hebdige associates *The Face* with the gentry, not ordinary citizens nor the working class. Still more important, he maps *The Face* onto a ubiquitous and imperial market economy in which processes of commodification befall everything. The blurring of distinctions and categories effected by market forces produces a surreal environment, making it difficult to hold faith in anything. In offering no resistance, undermining all norms, and celebrating liquefaction, *The Face* incurs the ire of Hebdige: it "capitulates symbolically to the empire of signs, robots, computers, miniaturisation and automobiles" (172). As such, it is "hyperconformist" (173).

For Hebdige *The Face* embodies and perpetuates a troubling sensibility characteristic of a certain historical conjuncture uniting consumer capitalism, Thatcherite conservatism, and postmodernism/poststructuralism. This conjuncture is regularly a target of Birmingham scholars. Some salient features of this sensibility include an obsession with shopping, a disdain for oppositional party politics, a weariness with older notions of community, and an end to judgment, meaning, and resisting subjectivity. What is perhaps most revealing here is the use of the concept of the mode of production (late or consumer capitalism) to explain the form taken by contemporary politics, philosophy, and media. In isolating *The Face* and mapping it onto various market forces, Hebdige resuscitates Marxist economism, forging links that foreground the class position and interests of the magazine. Like the conservative left critique of pop art, Hebdige's own criticism of *The Face* does not credit the iconoclastic power of the leveling of boundaries promoted by the magazine. At the point at which any such leveling undermines subjectivity, ethical and political normativity, and social activism, Hebdige draws a line and sides with traditional left humanistic values against postmodernism/ poststructuralism. The closing half of *Hiding in the Light* attacks poststructuralism, using as weapons caricature, hyperbole, and invective.

The poststructuralism/postmodernism that Hebdige deplores consists mainly of Baudrillard's post-Marxist work of the seventies and eighties. Little of substance is offered about Althusser, Derrida, Foucault, or Lacan. The early Barthes is mentioned appreciatively now and then. Deleuze and Guattari receive an occasional nod of approval. Lyotard is roundly criticized. Nothing much is said about feminist poststructuralists (Cixous, Kristeva, and others). The British poststructuralists associated with *Screen* and *Oxford Literary Review,* figured prominently in Easthope's history, are never mentioned, nor are American or other poststructuralists. The point is the "poststructuralism" attacked by Hebdige is severely truncated. It emerges at times as a monolithic nihilistic French nominalism deserving of measured scorn from sensible British empiricists/culturalists. Whereas the first half of *Hiding in the Light* offers memorable studies of cultural phenomena and objects (youth groups, rock stars, modes of design, scooters, cartoons, pop art, magazines), the second half degenerates at its worst moments into theoretical diatribe. The balance sought by Birmingham critics between culturalism and (post)structuralism is jeopardized as Hebdige relies upon a traditional humanism tinged with Marxism to extirpate poststructuralism.

It is common to equate "postmodernism" with postwar Western culture, which is characterized, in part, by a shift from a production-oriented to consumer-centered economic system. Often only the *new* elements and features of this historical era, not the whole era, are labelled "postmodern." According to this logic, poststructuralism, which is a new form of thought, is postmodern. However, to equate the two terms, as Hebdige and others do, is to exaggerate the reach of poststructuralism (one among a host of new movements) and to diminish the scope of postmodernism. Occasionally, Hebdige seems to be attacking an era when, in fact, he is criticizing one or two French poststructuralists. Confusion mars his endeavor here. Now and then

Baudrillard or Lyotard become whipping boys representative of much that is wrong in contemporary culture at large. The dubious totalizing representational practices used in this caricature at times produce drastically simplified allegories about the decadence of Western culture.

In Hebdige's most angry passages, poststructuralists/postmodernists occupy another world, a second planet. About this world, the milieu of *The Face,* he laments:

> There can be no "promiscuity" in a world without monogamy/monotheism/monadic subjects; there can be no "perversion" in a world without norms. (162)

> In this world, the vertical axis has collapsed. (159)

> We are left in a world of radically "empty" signifiers. No meaning. No classes. No history. (164)

> There is nowhere else to go but to the shops. For in a flat world there is an end, as well, to ideology. (168)

> Postmodernity is modernity without the hopes and dreams which made modernity bearable. (195)

> A no man's land which is just that: a land owned by no body . . . where questions of agency, cause, intention, authorship, history become irrelevant. (200)

> In the death of reason, the neophilia of the modern age gives way to the necrophilia and necro-mancy of the Post. (209)

> The discourse of postmodernism is fatal and fatalistic: at every turn the word "death" opens up to engulf us: "death of the subject," "death of the author," "death of art," "death of reason," "end of history." (210)

Against poststructuralism/postmodernism Hebdige seeks to restore a set of purportedly discredited categories, including certain hierarchies, hopes, dreams, intentions, and norms, and especially the concepts of reason, ownership, subjectivity, history, class, ideology, meaning, authorship, and art. Denouncing nihilism and fatalism, he offers affirmation and activism. Finally, he refutes the triple negation, said to be constitutive of poststructuralism, of utopianism, teleology, and totalization.

The attack on poststructuralism at times approaches hysteria, giving skimpy evidence of sustained and rigorous reading, insensitive to the life-enhancing thrust and the ethos of liberation frequently found in poststructuralist texts. The Derridean deconstruction of logocentrism is arguably as much a festive carnival as a wake. The same is true of Barthes's critical semiology, Deleuze's schizoanalysis, Kristeva's semanalysis, and Lyotard's paganism. The death of man announced by Foucault signals the end of the humanist conceptualization of so-called man, just as the death of the "author" proclaimed by Barthes declares the demise of the possessive and autonomous genius-father stemming from Renaissance humanism. Poststructuralism seeks to refigure "man" and "authorship," as well as "reason," "history," and "subjectivity." This is a wake primarily for those fiercely attached to the past and terrified of an uncertain future. That many poststructuralists are lapsed Marxists and emergent anarchists suspicious of party discipline is a main source of animus against them. Because poststructuralists sketch no political program, they are taken as advocates of resignation and fatalism. But the charge does not follow. The politics indirectly suggested by poststructuralists calls for micropolitical resistance and localized initiatives, not for quietism and retreat. However, by avoiding mass politics, poststructuralists open themselves to the charges of ineffectuality and quietism—accurate charges that are difficult to refute. It does not follow, though, that poststructuralists are necromancers.

In his introduction, Hebdige admits of his research on *The Face*, "In the end no one can really choose to live all the time on what I call in this article, 'Planets One' or 'Two.' Instead we are continually, all of us, being shuttled back and forth between them" (10). This oddly placed retraction confirms that Hebdige's portrait of poststructuralism/postmodernism tends toward exaggeration and caricature. In keeping with the distinctive effort of the CCCS to integrate British culturalism and French (post)structuralism, Hebdige observes, "It would be foolish to present a polar opposition between the Gramscian

line(s) and the (heterogeneous) Posts. There is too much shared historical and intellectual ground for such a partition to serve any valid purpose" (206). Indeed, there are many strands of poststructuralism, not
one: the bipolarity of "Two Planets" lacks pertinence as well as validity. Speaking pragmatically, Hebdige reveals in a note, "I have sought
to find a bottom line—a point of departure and return—from which
it becomes possible to draw on some poststructuralist, postmodernist
work" (254*n*). Of the arch postmodern/poststructuralist *The Face,* he
ultimately admits its superior aesthetic qualities (design, photogra-
phy, writing), its popular appeal and wide influence on other media,
and its progressive democratizing of knowledge and information.

The pattern of vacillation exhibited in the analyses of pop art and
The Face illustrates the difficulty Birmingham intellectuals, not just
Hebdige, have in accommodating poststructuralism. Perhaps most
problematic for them are the assaults on the humanistic conceptions
of subjectivity and experience, which for poststructuralists are discursive constructions cobbled together from linguistic codes and cultural
conventions imbricated within unconscious libidinal, historical, and
sociopolitical structures and practices. To the considerable extent to
which such concepts as agency, authorship, history, ideology, meaning, reason, and resistance depend upon the classical accounts of the
human subject and human experience, the poststructuralist deconstruction of both notions jeopardizes the enterprise of humanistic
cultural inquiry. What most challenges Birmingham critics is the
poststructuralist tendencies to atomize and relativize such cherished
analytical instruments. In this regard, the poststructuralist critiques
of teleology and totalization are particularly threatening, as Hebdige
makes clear. But, of course, poststructuralists regularly rely on large-
scale epochal assemblages like logocentrism, panopticism, *grands ré-
cits,* carceral networks, and phallogocentrism. It is not that poststructuralists eschew teleology and totalization, rather they are critical of
such operations. Partially justified, the anathema visited upon
poststructuralism by left humanists stems in large part from its negative critiques of traditional accounts of subjectivity and experience,
its inability to promulgate a political program and to promote revolu-

tionary activism, its suspicions of Marxist totalizing concepts, its tendency toward linguistic determinism, and its radical antihierarchalism often misconstrued as nihilism. Whatever the limitations of poststructuralism, the Marxist culturalism evident in CCCS research often bears only distant relations to classical Marxism and frequently seems as much poststructuralist as Marxist, a point to be discussed in a moment.

Crisis of Marxist Critique

The mid-eighties phenomenon of Band Aid, initiated by rock celebrities to help feed starving Third World people, gained massive public support via television, succeeding in constructing and mobilizing a new transnational community of ordinary people to reallocate resources through extragovernmental means. For this paradigmatic popular phenomenon, Hebdige has much praise. He notes that the vital networks created to feed the world operated "underneath the machinations of international finance capitalism, in the face of global domination of markets by multinational conglomerates and cartels," using "the most sophisticated communication technologies available, technologies developed more often than not to service the industrial-military complexes and to perpetuate their power" (216). Experienced with handling such technologies and creating affinities across ethnic, cultural, and national divisions, the leading rock musicians of Band Aid optimistically employed artistic and moral resources, "resuscitating traditions of co-operation, mutual assistance and that faith in human agency and collective action which had, for instance, animated the early trade unionists and the Labour Movement" (220). Not surprisingly, Hebdige values this event as a model of popular artists successfully linking aesthetics, economics, and politics through mass media to organize a macropolitical multi-ethnic global community dedicated to saving humankind. He has little tolerance for hostile criticism of Band Aid, and he is led to condemn the many critics, particularly those on the left, whose negativity so predominated as to inhibit appreciation of the positive potentialities of such populist phenomena as Band Aid.

To overcome the crisis of radical critique, Hebdige argues for more sustained attention to the complex consumption phases of cultural circuits, to what, following Grossberg, he calls "affective alliances." It is not a question of ignoring either form or production, but of more fully crediting the pragmatics and dialogics of cultural transactions. This receptionist focus is explicitly associated with the Gramscian line of the CCCS against the mandarin theoretical work of the Frank- furt school: "To engage with the popular as constructed and as lived . . . we are forced at once to desert the perfection of a purely theoreti- cal analysis, of a 'negative dialectic' (Adorno) in favour of a more 'sen- suous [and strategic] logic' (Gramsci)—a logic attuned to the living textures of popular culture, to the ebb and flow of popular debate" (203; Hebdige's brackets).

As Hebdige explains it, an "affective alliance" is an unpredictable and unstable coalition of heterogeneous national, racial, and sub- cultural groups formed into a counterhegemonic global community in response to such popular phenomena as punk, reggae, rap, Band Aid, Farm Aid, etc. "It no longer appears adequate to confine the ap- peal of these forms—the multiple lines of effect/affect emanating from them—to the ghetto of discrete, numerically small subcultures. For they permeate and help to organise a much broader, less bounded territory where cultures, subjectivities, identities, impinge upon each other" (212). Among various examples Hebdige offers the case of Bob Marley's Caribbean music and Rasta worldview that originate within a small group and spread via packaging, commercialization, and international communications to a hybrid global community of blacks in diaspora. Reggae music and its viewpoint summon up this community by abolishing geographical distances and local differences and by recalling a history of shared pain and deprivation. The power of the music and its themes reach dispossessed white youths, produc- ing a further "affective alliance" around the world of disaffected black and white youths.

Marxist radical critique would here typically adopt a different and negative stance, regarding affective alliances as capitalistic concoctions to expand markets. From this vantage Marley's use of rock guitar riffs, high-quality album sound, and the self-conscious dreadlocks-and-ganja image would amount to dilutions and deflections of resisting energies into commercial strategies. What Hebdige deplores is any doctrinaire negativity incapable of appreciating and assessing new political formations engendered through heterogeneous aesthetic forms and disseminated through mainstream circuits. Radical critique must not be blind to effectivity, affirmation, affectivity, joy. There is something other than authoritative and judgmental condemnation, self-cancellation, silencing.

Hebdige is critical of the early CCCS work, a considerable body of material, on subcultures. This turn manifests itself primarily as self-criticism, since Hebdige's own early work is frequently cited as exemplary of such subcultural inquiry. The Birmingham view of subcultures-as-negations, for instance of punk and reggae groups, stresses refusal, resistance, revolt and neglects celebration, confirmation, community. To overlook affective alliances is to restrict the reach of cultural circuits, limit the protocol of entanglement, miss spaces of collective intervention and positive action. Such anti-utopianism comports with the alleged fatalism of postmodernism/post-structuralism. It is evident to Hebdige that contemporary subcultural forms and values regularly combine in affective alliances, begetting heterogeneous macropolitical communities and instituting new cultural arenas for solidarity and transformation. Such alliances are neither simply sell-outs nor capitulations by subcultural groups.

Hebdige is no anarchist: he does not wish to escape or to disassemble overarching apparatuses of control constructed by states, corporations, or multinational complexes. He has little to say about such agencies of ideological (re)production as schools, courts, prisons, churches, hospitals, etc. What he does is to study in celebratory fashion certain creative and certain subversive uses of existing apparatuses and agencies. The stress on mechanisms of discipline and conformity, associated with Marxist institutional analysis and with Foucauldian inquiry, amounts to critique in a negative mode, which for Hebdige is blind to multiple affective alliances.

Hebdige is no revolutionary: he does not look to the day when the proletariat will revolt and take over governance. His interest is less in the working class per se or in particular disenfranchised subcultures than in alliances of ordinary citizens. About owning classes, elites, or the bourgeoisie, nothing systematic or substantive is said. Given the absence of class enemies, Hebdige's populism comes to embody affirmation without negativity at considerable cost, namely the virtual disappearance of life and death struggles, intractable separatisms, and violent exclusionary hierarchies. Accentuating the positive entails attenuating the negative.

Despite all his dramatic claims and declarations, Hebdige's populist politics appears at times more libertarian and poststructuralist than Gramscian and more post-Marxist than Marxian. This is true for others associated with the Birmingham Centre. Liquefaction does visit subjectivity, class, ideology, history, meaning, community; and instability, drifting, flux, chance, and mutability do rule the times.

> From the perspective heavily influenced by the Gramscian approach, nothing is anchored to the *grands récits,* to master narratives, to stable (positive) identities, to fixed and certain meanings: all social and semantic relations are contestable, hence mutable; everything appears to be in flux: there are no predictable outcomes. Though classes still exist, there is no guaranteed dynamic to class struggle and no "class belonging"; there are no solid homes to return to, no places reserved in advance for the righteous. No one "owns" an "ideology" because ideologies are themselves in process: in a state of constant formation and reformation. . . . There are only competing ideolog*ies,* themselves unstable constellations, liable to collapse at any moment into their component parts. These parts in turn can be recombined with other elements from other ideological formations to form fragile unities which in turn act to interpellate and bond together new imaginary communities, to forge fresh alliances between disparate social groups. (206–7)

For Hebdige the chancy alliances of social groups into new communities invariably constitute positive phenomena—objects worthy of cultural analysis rather than dismissive radical critique. The attack against the use of negation goes hand in hand with uncritical nostalgia for plebeian solidarity, unarticulated utopian aspirations for the populace, and an undermining of traditional radical concepts like class consciousness and ideology. Fragile coalitions replace proletarian revolutions; chance takes the place of planning; affective alliances supersede party discipline. All this appears closer to Baudrillard than Gramsci, nearer Foucault than Marx.

The shift of attention and allegiance from the working class to subcultures to the "populace" (composed of so-called ordinary people) transforms the Marxian legacy of the CCCS, as does the incorporation, reluctant or not, of numerous poststructuralist insights and concepts. The complex process of becoming post-Marxist shows up in the focus on middle-brow cultures as opposed to low- and high-brow cultures, and it manifests itself in the preoccupation with consumption and affectivity. (In the latter instance, to speak as a poststructuralist, CCCS work is concerned with the multivalent range of applications of items of popular culture, not with questions of misreading or linguistic duplicity. The regard for the pragmatics rather than the grammar or rhetoricity of plurisignation testifies to long-standing preferences for praxis over theory, politics over philosophy, sociology over linguistics.) Just as the populace consists of a plurality of porous groups, so the significance of cultural artifacts is tied to a plethora of outlets and uses. The linked concepts of cultural circuits and affective alliances instantiate the CCCS's most powerful version of the protocol of entanglement. In the end, however, the category "populace" (aggregate of ordinary people) emerges as a totalizing imaginary construct, a near-synonym for culture and society, an unstable and wishful sociopolitical formation too little affected by the bitter burdens of racial boundaries, gender restrictions, and national animosities. Denuded of much negativity, the notion of the "populace" does, nevertheless, enable a certain pluralistic project of cultural studies while it sustains the possibility of a macropolitics of counterhegemonic coalitions and alliances working through existing local and global cultural circuits. In such a setting, the popular arts, ranging from television, rock music, and movies to fashion, advertising, and magazines, have key political roles to play. Yet this idea of (wo)man en masse, transcending worldly obstacles, seems finally religious rather than political.

In Brantlinger's summative judgment, "While the Birmingham Centre has produced important, original results, its various attempts at theorization, exciting as these have sometimes been, have not moved much beyond what Williams, Hoggart, and Thompson originally offered" (163). From this resolutely culturalist point of view, the advent of poststructuralism has been a disaster. Hall, Johnson, and Hebdige, not to mention other CCCS intellectuals, ruin cultural studies by trying to cross it, however moderately, with poststructuralism. Brantlinger advocates a return to the three fathers and to Gramsci and Habermas. Given my own sympathy for poststructuralism, I regard the return to culturalism as a retreat, a retrograde effort to restore British empiricism and common sense against French semiotics and rationalism, trade-union Marxism against an emergent post-Marxism of populist coalitions, and heroic assertive selfhood against multiple contradictory subject-positions. In this context, the "crisis of radical critique," to use Hebdige's phrase, signals the turning point when the limits of Marxian analysis become evident in the face of the postmodern emergence of new subjectivities, political alignments, and affective alliances. Among cultural critics the call for culturalism today represents a call for discipline, defense, discipleship. It seeks a return to the 1950s. Hebdige is continuously attracted by this possibility, but finally he, like other Birmingham scholars, responds to poststructuralism, which reorients his thinking in spite of his caution and resistance.

CONCLUSION

Inside contemporary universities cultural criticism of various sorts is commonly practiced in programs of American studies, African-American studies, cultural studies, media and communication studies, and women's studies. Certain anthropologists, historians, and sociologists also employ cultural criticism. Within literary circles it constitutes something of a new frontier, though, of course, it has immediate precursors among philologists, cultural historians, Marxists, and myth critics, not to mention sometime New Critics like Eliot, Empson, Burke, and Winters. If there is a *new* cultural criticism, it is largely as a result of the arrival of "theory." Three examples illustrate this point. Gunn can present his project for a morally responsive and religiously oriented cultural criticism as "new" not because he revives Trilling and Burke but because he crosses them with Geertz and Bakhtin, producing a hybrid, however moderate. What is new about Jameson's cultural criticism is not the employment of Marxist concepts nor the deployment of accredited hermeneutical devices but the productive use of structuralist and poststructuralist insights grafted onto established Marxist and hermeneutical notions. Lentricchia's project for rhetoric is innovative largely insofar as it extends Burke to refute de Man, not insofar as it restores Burke, though the revival of a leftist Burke is overdue. Similar observations can be made about Eagleton's rhetoric, Said's secular criticism, Scholes's textual studies, and the new historicists' various enterprises. Several points need emphasis. While cultural criticism has been practiced for several centuries, the recent advent of "theory" has revitalized and transformed it. In this context, my own project seeks not to restore forerunners of cultural criticism, but to illustrate the weak points of influential predecessors, cultural critics and otherwise, showing how poststructuralism offers useful supplements to reigning modes of critical inquiry.

It might be worth pointing out that what is called new historicism is a turn toward sociological, political, and historical criticism, indebted to structuralism and poststructuralism, particularly Foucault, manifested first during the late 1970s in the writings of Greenblatt, Lentricchia, Said, and others; it is not, as some theorists believe, a movement limited to those at the University of California-Berkeley associated with the journal *Representations*. As my comments on these figures suggest, I am sympathetic toward new historicism, though not without specific reservations about each figure. I subscribe to the charter of new historicism outlined by Veeser (xi): discourse is embedded in networks of material practices; critique employs methods it risks falling prey to; literary and nonliterary texts circulate inseparably; discourse provides access to neither eternal truths nor stable human nature; cultural criticism under capitalist conditions (or any other conditions) participates in economy. Nonetheless, new historicists tend to keep alive much of the legacy and practice of traditional humanism, which some of its critics demonstrate (see Veeser).

As is well known, certain cultural critics in the academy have come increasingly to promote the development of the emergent field of cultural studies. At some universities there are centers and institutes of cultural studies and at others interdepartmental and intradepartmental programs and tracks (graduate and undergraduate). These sites provide institutional spaces where typically teachers and students work together from such areas as anthropology, ethnic studies, film and television studies, history, literary theory, political theory, popular culture, postcolonial studies, rhetoric, sociology, and women's studies. It would be no surprise if cultural studies in the United States continued developing into a separate discipline, as it already has in Britain and elsewhere, complete with autonomous departments and national and regional organizations. Significant programs, journals, and university press series have appeared and promise to continue doing so. In this connection, the project of cultural criticism outlined in this book can function in the emerging area of cultural studies as well as in traditional branches of literary studies. Scholars working with, say, Renaissance texts need not flee English or foreign language departments nor await the institutionalization of the discipline of cultural studies to practice cultural criticism.

*   *   *

Because the vanguard work carried out at Birmingham's Centre for Contemporary Cultural Studies serves as the leading model for contemporary cultural criticism, I want to comment briefly on several aspects of Richard Johnson's watershed report summarizing and synthesizing the CCCS project. Johnson and others accurately characterize the Centre's methodological endeavor as a grafting of French poststructuralist thought onto a leftist empiricist British tradition. Weaving together these two modes, Johnson constructs an ambitious suggestive model for cultural studies that illustrates the circuits through which cultural practices and products move in the stages of production, distribution, and consumption (see figure A. 1). According to the model, the conditions of both cultural creation and interpretation involve concrete, particular, private lives and abstract, "universal," public representations. While the forms of texts are public, the social relations of lived cultures are private. Johnson's main argument is that "each box represents a moment in this circuit. Each moment or aspect depends upon the others and is indispensable to the whole. . . . It follows that if we are placed at one point of the circuit, we do not necessarily see what is happening at others" (46). The primary methodological purpose of the diagram is to schematize the entire process, warn against the dangers of partial perspectives, and encourage collaborative work on each of the four phases.

There are some telling problems with this bold model. In particular, the organizing private/public opposition repeats the traditional false separation of experience from discourse. Purportedly, there is a public realm of forms and representations that are abstract and "universal," and there is a distinguishable private realm of social lives that are concrete and particular. Despite his attention to poststructuralism, Johnson here refuses its linguistic understanding of semiotic activity. Specifically, the constitution of the subject—the so-called private life—entails entry by means of discourse into symbolic realms. There is no private life unmarked by public discourse. Presence is al-

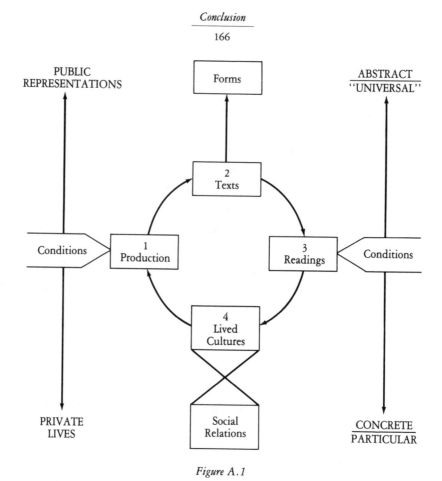

Figure A.1

Circuit of Cultural Products

ways representation. In Derridean terms, there is no getting around the inscriptions of writing and their intertextual sedimentations. To come into consciousness is to take on a name, a body, an unconscious, a gender role, a family, a religion, an education. Public institutions shape "private" subjectivity. From the outset cultural forms mold life and experience. Johnson's diagram has certain things wrong. The top layer of the chart could be transposed to the bottom to show that public representations constitute private lives and that abstract "universal" conventions underlie concrete particular practices. Moreover, for literary intellectuals the whole idea that creative production generates textual forms that undergo readings is a discredited fiction: the writing of a work entails the creative misreading of predecessors, that is, reading forms part of literary production and, in addition, critical interpretation consists of (re)writing texts. Thus, the separation into distinct phases of production and consumption collapses, showing production as a mode of consumption and consumption as a mode of production.

Much valuable and provocative scholarly work has, of course, come out of the CCCS. In Anglophone countries it is an undisputed pioneer of contemporary cultural criticism and cultural studies. Some basic formulations can be extrapolated from CCCS work. Cultural criticism seeks to avoid the belletristic and formalistic habits of isolating and monumentalizing aesthetic works. To sacralize is to deracinate and mummify. The aesthetic is not limited to the classic but includes the common. The task of cultural criticism is to analyze and assess the social roots, institutional relays, and ideological ramifications of communal events, institutions, and texts. Against the weakening but still regnant scholarly focus on aesthetic masterpieces of canonized high literature, cultural criticism advances the claims of "low," working-class, marginal, popular, minority, and mass cultural discourses.

*   *   *

Among many contemporary cultural critics the conservative stance of the traditional intellectual as disinterested connoisseur and custodian of culture is regarded as unacceptable. The literature by cultural theorists on the possible roles of intellectuals is extensive and growing (see, for example, Barthes, Bourdieu, Bové, Brenkman, Foucault, Giroux et al., Gramsci, Jameson, Kristeva, Lentricchia, Merod, Ohmann, Ryan, and Said). To cast the critic as a preserver of the status quo is to limit the function of criticism to reproduction of the established order. "Criticism" as explication and not critique is criticism unworthy of the name. In pedagogical arenas, criticism is still widely called upon to initiate students into accepted mainstream middle-class values and practices. The mass production by universities of docile yet competent persons approaches being indoctrination within a carceral system. Pedagogy needs to promote student experience with heterogeneous social groups, democratic decision making, popular culture, canon revaluation, multiple literacies, classroom deregimentation, and cultural alternatives. Significantly, the many attacks in recent years against the conservative politics of normal criticism and pedagogy, especially those mounted by feminist and black intellectuals, have established more or less tolerated spheres of oppositional and resisting criticism within universities. And it is here that cultural critique has been developed and disseminated beyond tiny enclaves, though campaigns against so-called political correctness seek to roll back such advances.

In my understanding, intellectuals are situated amid determining historical, social, and political matrices that proffer vocational patterns sanctioned by society. Within regimes of reason, conformity and resistance are alike coded. Still, regimes of reason are sites of contestation always in process of formation, having multiple shifting margins and pockets of resistance, which can be linked at certain moments and places in oppositional coalitions. The porousness and spotty openness of regimes at any and every given time and place engender conditions more or less favorable to productive intellectual activity—to inquiry, scholarship, resistance, leadership, student empowerment, opposition, change. Being subject to "reason" does not involve thoroughgoing subjection, although the positions of intellectuals are characteristically constrained by whole complexes of circumstances related to existing regimes. The complicated bottom line is that academic intellectuals are intricately and inescapably implicated in regimes of unreason, that they can more or less unwittingly serve the established order both by attempting to avoid it and to criticize it, and that they can, nevertheless, transform it.

The location of university intellectuals is such that "self"-reflection requires multifaceted analysis of the processes of cultural regimentation, the resources of cultural critique, and the possibilities for change. Adorno's despairing postwar thoughts on such matters merit consideration: "The cultural critic is not happy with civilization, to which alone he owes his discontent. He speaks as if he represented either unadulterated nature or a higher historical stage. Yet he is necessarily of the same essence as that to which he fancies himself superior. . . . The subject itself is mediated down to its innermost make-up by the notion to which it opposes itself as independent and sovereign" (19). In Adorno's view, the cultural critic is culture's "salaried and honoured nuisance," a figure "measured only in terms of his marketable success" (20). In the end, therefore, "even the most radical reflection of the mind on its own failure is limited by the fact that it remains only reflection, without altering the existence to which its failure bears witness" (32–33). Significantly, Adorno locates cultural critics firmly within monolithic modern regimes of reason characterized by ubiquitous technical rationality and omnipotent market economies, which commodify all entities and relations, thoroughly reifying existence. The terms set by market rationality coopt cultural critics who, in reaction, seek to embrace avant-garde utopian negativities as critical freedom.

Adorno constructs an unmodulated totalizing view of cultural regimentation, ignoring multiple sites of resistance and spaces for critique and change. Hebdige's youth subcultures and affective alliances offer counterevidence, as do the many successes of oppositional minority groups. Adorno's legendary disdain for popular culture and his blindness to new social movements limit the pertinence of his portrait of cultural criticism and cultural change. Culture, as Cottom reminds us, is always a concocted *imaginary* totality. Against Adorno I would argue that modern "cultures" typically consist of numerous contending groups, defined variously by class, race, ethnicity, gender, religion, dialect, and nationality, and, furthermore, that most individuals hold memberships in several such groups. In short, modern cultures are fragmented along multiple lines, opening opportune sites for critique and transformation in the pursuit of equality, reciprocity, polylogue, power-sharing, difference, tolerance, nonviolence, decentralization, and liberation.

*   *   *

I would like to conclude by mulling over various meanings of "culture." There is a broad tendency to conceive "culture" as a realm of ornamentation, ritual, and belief built atop "society" with its basic means and methods of production. Such a superstructure/

infrastructure model renders "culture" an epiphenomenal by-product of "society." In more or less dropping the term *society* and using mainly the word *culture,* I aim not simply to equate the two but to harness the connotations of "constructedness" and "difference" that generally accompany "culture" and not "society." Where "culture" is a lexical neighbor of choice and variety, "society" is a semantic conscript of fate and necessity. The constructedness of "culture" suggests the arbitrariness and transformability of human arrangements, both past and present. It is a question of de-absolutizing "social" determinism, not of denying it. To declare that a cultural critic studies "cultural formations," therefore, is different than proclaiming that such a critic studies "social formations." The former declaration implies attention to constitutive discursive codes, institutional norms, and hegemonic and oppositional practices, whereas the latter suggests distanced empirical observation of inert entities.

In Williams's thoughts on keywords, "culture" comes positively to designate a "central formation of values" and a "particular way of life" (12). This influential formulation subtly covers over differences, fragmentations, hostilities, and challenges. The very ideas of "central formation" and "particular way" intimate, yet discount, other contending "formations" and "ways." In decentering and pluralizing such concepts of "culture," one steps back to less grandiose notions focused on concatenations of communities that are disparate, local, different. The next step is to detotalize the relatively homogeneous idea of "community" in the name of the heterogeneity of subgroups and individuals. The final step is to deconstruct the subject that is fissured by an (inaccessible) unconscious, that is in process, and that is continuously interpellated into and shaped by cultures. Ultimately, there is no escaping culture, yet multiple differences and resistances exist in every sphere and at every level, illustrating that culture is an unstable metaphorical construct more or less open to differential analysis and transformation.

I prefer to employ "regimes of reason" rather than "culture," "society," or "ideology," when referring to the activities of cultural criticism, because this concept suggests arbitrariness and instability, solidity and discipline, institutional power and knowledge. What constitutes "reason" is open to question and challenge. A "regime" is a contestable formation. Still, to challenge or change a regime decisively is a considerable undertaking given its scope, complexity, reach, inertia, networks of institutions, rationalizations of interests, and systems of safeguards. To analyze and critique cultural texts in light of regimes of reason/unreason is to confront multiple, sometimes undecidable elements of both fragile contingency and solid monumentality, all historically formed, politically weighted, and institutionally situated, enacting inclusions and exclusions and privileging some "things" over others. In the end, intervening in regimes of reason constitutes the primary intellectual ethicopolitical work of cultural criticism.

REFERENCES

Adorno, Theodor W. "Cultural Criticism and Society." In *Prisms*, translated by Samuel Weber and Shierry Weber, pp. 19–34. London: Spearman, 1967.

Althusser, Louis. *Lenin and Philosophy and Other Essays*, translated by Ben Brewster. New York: Monthly Review Press, 1971.

Attridge, Derek, Geoff Bennington, and Robert Young, eds. *Post-Structuralism and the Question of History*. New York: Cambridge University Press, 1987.

Baker, Houston A., Jr. *Long Black Song: Essays in Black American Literature and Culture*. Charlottesville: University Press of Virginia, 1972.

Bakhtin, M. M. *The Dialogic Imagination: Four Essays*, edited by Michael Holquist, translated by Caryl Emerson and Michael Holquist. Austin: University of Texas Press, 1981.

Baraka, Amiri [LeRoi Jones]. *Home: Social Essays*. New York: William Morrow, 1966.

Barthes, Roland. "The Death of the Author." In *Image—Music—Text*, edited and translated by Stephen Heath, pp. 142–48. New York: Hill and Wang, 1977.

———. *Mythologies*, translated by Annette Lavers. New York: Noonday, 1972.

———. *S/Z*, translated by Richard Miller. New York: Hill and Wang, 1974.

———. "Writers, Intellectuals, Teachers." In *Image—Music—Text*, pp. 190–215.

Batsleer, Janet, et al. *Rewriting English: Cultural Politics of Gender and Class*. London: Methuen, 1985.

Baudrillard, Jean. *The Mirror of Production*, translated by Mark Poster. St. Louis: Telos, 1975.

Bhabha, Homi K. "The Commitment to Theory." *New Formations* 5 (Summer 1988):5–23.

Blackmur, R. P. "A Critic's Job of Work." In *Language as Gesture: Essays in Poetry*, pp. 372–99. New York: Harcourt, 1952.

Bleich, David. *Readings and Feelings: An Introduction to Subjective Criticism*. Urbana, Ill.: National Council of Teachers of English, 1975.

Bloom, Harold. *The Anxiety of Influence: A Theory of Poetry.* New York: Oxford University Press, 1973.

———. *A Map of Misreading.* New York: Oxford University Press, 1975.

Booth, Wayne. *Critical Understanding: The Powers and Limits of Pluralism.* Chicago: University of Chicago Press, 1979.

Bourdieu, Pierre. *Distinction: A Social Critique of the Judgment of Taste,* translated by Richard Nice. Cambridge: Harvard University Press, 1984.

———. *Homo Academicus,* translated by Peter Collier. Stanford: Stanford University Press, 1988.

Bové, Paul A. *Intellectuals in Power: A Genealogy of Critical Humanism.* New York: Columbia University Press, 1986.

Brantlinger, Patrick. *Crusoe's Footprints: Cultural Studies in Britain and America.* New York: Routledge, 1990.

Brenkman, John. *Culture and Domination.* Ithaca: Cornell University Press, 1987.

Brooks, Cleanth. "The Heresy of Paraphrase." In *The Well Wrought Urn: Studies in the Structure of Poetry,* pp. 176–96. New York: Reynal and Hitchcock, 1947.

Burke, Kenneth. "Formalist Criticism: Its Principles and Limits." In *Language as Symbolic Action: Essays on Life, Literature, and Method,* pp. 480–506. Berkeley: University of California Press, 1966.

Cain, William E. *The Crisis in Criticism: Theory, Literature, and Reform in English Studies.* Baltimore: Johns Hopkins University Press, 1984.

Centre for Contemporary Cultural Studies. *Culture, Media, Language: Working Papers in Cultural Studies, 1972–1979.* London: Hutchinson, 1980.

———. *Resistance Through Rituals: Youth Subcultures in Post-War Britain.* London: Hutchinson, 1976.

Christian, Barbara. *Black Feminist Criticism: Perspectives on Black Women Writers.* New York: Pergamon, 1985.

Cixous, Hélène. "The Laugh of the Medusa." In *New French Feminisms: An Anthology,* edited by Elaine Marks and Isabelle de Courtivron, pp. 245–64. New York: Schocken, 1981.

Corlett, William. *Community without Unity: A Politics of Derridian Extravagance.* Durham: Duke University Press, 1989.

Cottom, Daniel. *Text and Culture: The Politics of Interpretation.* Minneapolis: University of Minnesota Press, 1989.

Crane, R. S. *The Idea of the Humanities and Other Essays Critical and Historical,* vol. 2. Chicago: University of Chicago Press, 1967.

Culler, Jonathan. *On Deconstruction: Theory and Criticism after Structuralism.* Ithaca: Cornell University Press, 1982.

————. *Structuralist Poetics: Structuralism, Linguistics and the Study of Litera-ture*. Ithaca: Cornell University Press, 1975.

de Certeau, Michel. *The Practice of Everyday Life*, translated by Steven Ren-dall. Berkeley: University of California Press, 1984.

Deleuze, Gilles, and Félix Guattari. *Kafka: Toward a Minor Literature*, trans-lated by Dana Polan. Minneapolis: University of Minnesota Press, 1986.

de Man, Paul. *Allegories of Reading: Figural Language in Rousseau, Nietzsche, Rilke, and Proust*. New Haven: Yale University Press, 1979.

————. *Blindness and Insight: Essays in the Rhetoric of Contemporary Criticism*, 2d rev. ed. Minneapolis: University of Minnesota Press, 1983.

————. "Shelley Disfigured." In *Deconstruction and Criticism*, edited by Harold Bloom et al., pp. 39–73. New York: Seabury, 1979.

Derrida, Jacques. *Dissemination*, translated by Barbara Johnson. Chicago: University of Chicago Press, 1981.

————. *Of Grammatology*, translated by Gayatri Chakravorty Spivak. Bal-timore: Johns Hopkins University Press, 1976.

Eagleton, Terry. *Literary Theory: An Introduction*. Minneapolis: University of Minnesota Press, 1983.

Easthope, Antony. *British Post-Structuralism Since 1968*. London: Routledge, 1988.

Fanon, Frantz. *The Wretched of the Earth*, translated by Constance Farrington. New York: Grove, 1963.

Felman, Shoshana. "Rereading Femininity." *Yale French Studies*, Special Issue on "Feminist Readings: French Texts/American Contexts." 62 (1981):19–44.

Fish, Stanley E. *Is There a Text in This Class? The Authority of Interpretive Com-munities*. Cambridge: Harvard University Press, 1980.

Foucault, Michel. *Discipline and Punish: The Birth of the Prison*, translated by Alan Sheridan. New York: Vintage, 1979.

————. "Truth and Power." In *Power/Knowledge: Selected Interviews and Other Writings 1972–77*, edited by Colin Gordon, translated by Colin Gordon et al., pp. 109–33. New York: Pantheon, 1980.

————. "What Is An Author?" In *Language, Counter-Memory, Practice: Se-lected Essays and Interviews*, edited by Donald F. Bouchard, translated by D. F. Bouchard and Sherry Simon, pp. 113–38. Ithaca: Cornell University Press, 1977.

Frye, Northrop. *Anatomy of Criticism: Four Essays*. Princeton: Princeton Uni-versity Press, 1957.

Gates, Henry Louis, Jr. "Criticism in the Jungle." In *Black Literature and Literary Theory*, edited by H. L. Gates, Jr., pp. 1–24. New York: Meth-uen, 1984.

Gayle, Addison, Jr., ed. *The Black Aesthetic.* Garden City, N.Y.: Anchor, 1971.

Gilbert, Sandra M., and Susan Gubar. *The Madwoman in the Attic: The Woman Writer and the Nineteenth-Century Literary Imagination.* New Haven: Yale University Press, 1979.

Giroux, Henry, David Shumway, Paul Smith, and James Sosnoski. "The Need for Cultural Studies: Resisting Intellectuals and Oppositional Public Spheres." *Dalhousie Review* 64 (Summer 1984):472–86.

Graff, Gerald. *Professing Literature: An Institutional History.* Chicago: University of Chicago Press, 1987.

Gramsci, Antonio. *Selections from the Prison Notebooks,* edited and translated by Quintin Hoare and Geoffrey Nowell Smith. New York: International Publishers, 1971.

Green, Michael. "The Centre for Contemporary Cultural Studies." In *Re-Reading English,* edited by Peter Widdowson, pp. 77–90. London: Methuen, 1982.

Greenblatt, Stephen. *Renaissance Self-Fashioning: From More to Shakespeare.* Chicago: University of Chicago Press, 1980.

Grossberg, Lawrence. "The Circulation of Cultural Studies." *Critical Studies in Mass Communication* 6 (1989):413–20.

———. "Cultural Studies Revisited and Revised." In *Communications in Transition: Issues and Debates in Current Research,* edited by Mary S. Mander, pp. 39–70. New York: Praeger, 1983.

———. "The Formation of Cultural Studies: An American in Birmingham." *Strategies* 2 (1989):114–48.

———. "History, Politics and Postmodernism: Stuart Hall and Cultural Studies." *Journal of Communication Inquiry,* Special Issue on Stuart Hall, 10 (1986):61–77.

Grossberg, Lawrence, Cary Nelson, and Paula Treichler, eds. *Cultural Studies.* New York: Routledge, 1992.

Gunn, Giles. *The Culture of Criticism and the Criticism of Culture.* New York: Oxford University Press, 1987.

Hall, Stuart. "Cultural Studies: Two Paradigms." In *Culture, Ideology and Social Process: A Reader,* edited by Tony Bennett et al., pp. 19–37. London: Open University Press, 1981.

Harari, Josué V., ed. *Textual Strategies: Perspectives in Post-Structuralist Criticism.* Ithaca: Cornell University Press, 1979.

Harlow, Barbara. *Resistance Literature.* New York: Methuen, 1987.

Hartman, Geoffrey H. *Criticism in the Wilderness: The Study of Literature Today.* New Haven: Yale University Press, 1980.

Hebdige, Dick. *Hiding in the Light: On Images and Things.* London: Routledge, 1988.

——. *Subculture: The Meaning of Style.* New York: Methuen, 1979.

Henderson, Stephen. "Introduction: The Forms of Things Unknown." In *Understanding the New Black Poetry: Black Speech and Black Music as Poetic References,* pp. 3–69. New York: William Morrow, 1973.

Heuermann, Hartmut, ed. *Classics in Cultural Criticism II: U.S.A.* Frankfurt am Main: Peter Lang, 1990.

Hirsch, E. D., Jr. *Validity in Interpretation.* New Haven: Yale University Press, 1967.

Hoggart, Richard. "Schools of English and Contemporary Society." In *Speaking to Each Other,* vol. 2, pp. 246–59. New York: Oxford University Press, 1970.

Howe, Florence. *Myths of Coeducation: Selected Essays, 1964–1983.* Bloomington: Indiana University Press, 1984.

Howe, Irving. *Politics and the Novel.* New York: Horizon, 1957.

Jakobson, Roman. "Linguistics and Poetics." In *Language in Literature,* edited by Krystyna Pomorska and Stephen Rudy, pp. 62–94. Cambridge: Harvard University Press, 1987.

Jameson, Fredric. *Marxism and Form: Twentieth-Century Dialectical Theories of Literature.* Princeton: Princeton University Press, 1971.

——. *The Political Unconscious: Narrative as a Socially Symbolic Act.* Ithaca: Cornell University Press, 1981.

JanMohamed, Abdul R. *Manichean Aesthetics: The Politics of Literature in Colonial Africa.* Amherst: University of Massachusetts Press, 1983.

JanMohamed, Abdul R., and David Lloyd. "Introduction: Minority Discourse—What Is to Be Done?" *Cultural Critique,* Special Issue on "The Nature and Context of Minority Discourse II," 7 (Fall 1987):5–17.

Johnson, Barbara. *A World of Difference.* Baltimore: Johns Hopkins University Press, 1987.

Johnson, Lesley. *The Cultural Critics.* Boston: Routledge & Kegan Paul, 1979.

Johnson, Richard. "What Is Cultural Studies Anyway?" *Social Text* 16 (1986–87):38–80.

Krieger, Murray. *Arts on the Level: The Fall of the Elite Object.* Knoxville: University of Tennessee Press, 1981.

Kristeva, Julia. "A New Type of Intellectual: The Dissident." In *The Kristeva Reader,* edited by Toril Moi, pp. 292–300. New York: Columbia University Press, 1986.

——. *Revolution in Poetic Language,* translated by Margaret Waller. New York: Columbia University Press, 1984.

Kroeber, Alfred Louis, and Clyde Kluckhohn. *Culture: A Critical Review of Concepts and Definitions*. Cambridge, Mass.: Peabody Museum, 1952.

Lacan, Jacques. *Écrits: A Selection*, translated by Alan Sheridan. New York: Norton, 1977.

Laclau, Ernesto, and Chantal Mouffe. *Hegemony and Socialist Strategy: Towards A Radical Democratic Politics*. London: Verso, 1985.

Lange, Bernd-Peter, ed. *Classics in Cultural Criticism I: Britain*. Frankfurt am Main: Peter Lang, 1990.

Leitch, Vincent B. *American Literary Criticism from the Thirties to the Eighties*. New York: Columbia University Press, 1988.

———. "Cultural Criticism." *New Princeton Encyclopedia of Poetry and Poetics*, 3d ed., edited by Alex Preminger and T. V. F. Brogan, pp. 262–64. Princeton: Princeton University Press, 1993.

———. "Deconstruction and Ethics. Review of *Versions of Pygmalion*, by J. Hillis Miller." *Comparative Literature* 44 (Spring 1992):200–6.

———. *Deconstructive Criticism*. New York: Columbia University Press, 1983.

———. "Postmodern Culture: The Ambivalence of Fredric Jameson. Review of *Postmodernism or the Logic of Late Capitalism*, by Fredric Jameson." *College Literature* 19 (June 1992): 111–22.

Lentricchia, Frank. *Criticism and Social Change*. Chicago: University of Chicago Press, 1983.

Lyotard, Jean-François. *The Differend: Phrases in Dispute*, translated by Georges Van Den Abbeele. Minneapolis: University of Minnesota Press, 1988.

McRobbie, Angela. "New Times in Cultural Studies." Working Papers, Center for Twentieth-Century Studies, 5 (Fall/Winter 1990–91).

Mailloux, Steven. *Interpretive Conventions*. Ithaca: Cornell University Press, 1982.

Merod, Jim. *The Political Responsibility of the Critic*. Ithaca: Cornell University Press, 1987.

Miller, J. Hillis. *The Ethics of Reading: Kant, de Man, Eliot, Trollope, James, and Benjamin*. Wellek Library Lectures 5. New York: Columbia University Press, 1987.

Millett, Kate. *Sexual Politics*. Garden City, N.Y.: Doubleday, 1970.

Neal, Larry. "The Black Arts Movement." *tdr: The Drama Review* 12 (Summer 1968):29–39.

Nelson, Cary, and Lawrence Grossberg, ed. *Marxism and the Interpretation of Culture*. Urbana: University of Illinois Press, 1988.

Ohmann, Richard. *English in America: A Radical View of the Profession*. New York: Oxford University Press, 1976.

Olson, Elder. "A Dialogue on Symbolism." In *Critics and Criticism: Ancient and Modern*, edited by R. S. Crane, pp. 567–94. Chicago: University of Chicago Press, 1952.

Parry, Benita. "Problems in Current Theories of Colonial Discourse." *Oxford Literary Review* 9 (1987):27–58.

Peck, Jeffrey M. "Advanced Literary Study as Cultural Study: A Redefinition of the Discipline." In *Profession 85*, edited by Phyllis Franklin and Richard Brod, pp. 49–54. New York: Modern Language Association, 1985.

Poulet, Georges. "Phenomenology of Reading." *New Literary History* 1 (October 1969):53–68.

Pratt, Mary Louise. "Interpretive Strategies/Strategic Interpretations: On Anglo-American Reader-Response Criticism." *Boundary 2* 11 (Fall/Winter 1982–1983):201–31.

Ransom, John Crowe. "Poetry: A Note in Ontology." In *The World's Body*, pp. 111–42. 1938. Reprint. Baton Rouge: Louisiana State University Press, 1968.

Richards, I. A. *Science and Poetry.* New York: Norton, 1926.

Riffaterre, Michael. "Describing Poetic Structures: Two Approaches to Baudelaire's 'Les Chats.'" In *Structuralism*, edited by Jacques Ehrmann, pp. 188–230. Garden City, N.Y.: Doubleday, 1970.

Rosmarin, Adena. *The Power of Genre.* Minneapolis: University of Minnesota Press, 1985.

Ryan, Michael. *Politics and Culture: Working Hypotheses for a Post-Revolutionary Society.* Baltimore: Johns Hopkins University Press, 1989.

Said, Edward W. *Orientalism.* New York: Vintage, 1978.

Scholes, Robert. *Protocols of Reading.* New Haven: Yale University Press, 1989.

———. *Textual Power: Literary Theory and the Teaching of English.* New Haven: Yale University Press, 1985.

Showalter, Elaine. *A Literature of Their Own: British Women Novelists from Brontë to Lessing.* Princeton: Princeton University Press, 1977.

Smith, Barbara. "Toward a Black Feminist Criticism." In *The New Feminist Criticism: Essays on Women, Literature, and Theory*, edited by Elaine Showalter, pp. 168–85. New York: Pantheon, 1985.

Smith, Barbara Herrnstein. *Contingencies of Value: Alternative Perspectives for Critical Theory.* Cambridge: Harvard University Press, 1988.

Spivak, Gayatri Chakravorty. *In Other Worlds: Essays in Cultural Politics.* New York: Methuen, 1987.

Taine, H. A. *History of English Literature*, translated by H. Van Laun. 2 vols. New York: Henry Holt, 1874.

Thompson, E. P. *The Making of the English Working Class.* New York: Vintage, 1963.

Todorov, Tzvetan. *The Fantastic: A Structural Approach to a Literary Genre,* translated by Richard Howard. Ithaca: Cornell University Press, 1975.

Turner, Graeme. *British Cultural Studies: An Introduction.* Boston: Unwin Hyman, 1990.

Veeser, H. Aram, ed. *The New Historicism.* New York: Routledge, 1989.

Webster, Grant. *The Republic of Letters: A History of Postwar American Literary Opinion.* Baltimore: Johns Hopkins University Press, 1979.

Wellek, René, and Austin Warren. *Theory of Literature,* 3d ed. New York: Harcourt, 1962.

Wheelwright, Philip. *The Burning Fountain: A Study in the Language of Symbolism.* Bloomington: Indiana University Press, 1954.

White, Hayden. *Metahistory: The Historical Imagination in Nineteenth-Century Europe.* Baltimore: Johns Hopkins University Press, 1973.

———. *Tropics of Discourse: Essays in Cultural Criticism.* Baltimore: Johns Hopkins University Press, 1978.

Williams, Raymond. *Culture and Society 1780–1950.* London: Penguin, 1958.

———. *Keywords: A Vocabulary of Culture and Society.* New York: Oxford University Press, 1976.

———. "The Uses of Cultural Theory." *New Left Review* 158 (July/August 1986): 19–36.

Willis, Paul. *Learning to Labour: How Working Class Kids Get Working Class Jobs.* New York: Columbia University Press, 1977.

Wimsatt, W. K., Jr., and Monroe C. Beardsley. "The Intentional Fallacy." In *The Verbal Icon: Studies in the Meaning of Poetry,* pp. 3–18. Lexington: University of Kentucky Press, 1954.

Wimsatt, W. K., Jr., and Cleanth Brooks. *Literary Criticism: A Short History.* 1957. Reprint. Chicago: University of Chicago Press, 1978.

Young, Robert, ed. *Untying the Text: A Post-Structuralist Reader.* Boston: Routledge & Kegan Paul, 1981.

INDEX